GUNS, DRUGS, GANGS, & ANGER

GUNS, DRUGS, GANGS, & ANGER

Alvin S. Woods

Edited by
Mike Valentino

MOTOWN PUBLISHING
Detroit, Michigan

GUNS, DRUGS, GANGS, & ANGER

LIBRARY OF CONGRESS CATALOGING –IN-PUBLICATION DATA IS AVAILABLE.

ISBN 978-0-615-74116-1

Motown Publishing
P.O. Box 19612.
Detroit, Michigan 48219

Printed in the United States of America

This book is dedicated to change, the way we see each other, the way we treat each other, the way we love each other. It was not written for the intent of profit, but to help bring a needed change. The intent of the author is to give this book to those in need of the information before making the wrong choices in life that lead to crime and shorter lives.

Copies of this book can be ordered on the author page at www.gunsandanger.com or by calling the publisher directly at 313/310-1664 or 248/890-1664.

You may also contact the publisher at:
Motown Publishing
P.O. Box 19612
Detroit, Michigan 48219

Acknowledgements

First, I give glory and thanks to God for the many years some said I would not see. Thank you for the wisdom.

Next, I thank my wife Marie for many years of supporting my ideas and aspirations. Your inspiration has played a great part in my success. Thank you most for the love and believing in me.

Thanks to all my family and children who have kept me alive in spirit. Thanks for letting me know what it feels like to be royalty. I am one of the most proud dads that ever lived.

Much love to my sister Deborah Woods (Ebony) for the recollections and taking the time and spending hours to give me the editorial critiques that helped this project be a more successful one.

Thanks to the Satan's Sidekicks M/C, for their blessings of a successful project.

I give honor to my friend and well-respected elder and author Dr. John Telford who took time to prepare the foreword of this book. Thanks for the decades of dedication to the Detroit Public Schools and the students. We thank you.

My final acknowledgment is the greatest and goes to a gentleman I met named Bob Brown back in the early nineties while working as a skycap at Detroit's Metro Airport. Upon learning I had a desire to write, briefly knowingly me as a job acquaintance presented me with a book that he took time to shop for. The name of it was _The Artist's Way_, by Julia Cameron. Though the spiritual enlightening in the book was timely, it wasn't until I discovered the words he wrote to me on the last pages were more thoughtful than the entire book. And because there are many with the same desires I had, I feel obligated to share his words with all.

"Years ago, a young man in London aspired to be a writer, but everything seemed to be against him. He had never been able to attend school more than five years. His father had been flung in jail because he could not pay his debts, and this young man often knew the pangs of hunger. Finally he got a job pasting labels on bottle backings in a rat-infested whorehouse. He slept at night in a dismal attic room with two other boys – gutter swipes from the slums of London. He had so little confidence in his ability to write that he sneaked out and mailed (in the dead of night) his first manuscript, so nobody would laugh at him! Story after story was refused. Finally the great day came when one was accepted. True, he wasn't paid a shilling for it, but one editor had praised him. One editor had given him recognition. He was so thrilled that he wandered aimlessly around the streets with tears in his eyes rolling down his cheeks

The Praise, the recognition that he received by getting one story in print, changed his life. For if it had not been for that encouragement, he might have spent his entire life working in rat-infested factories.

Your may have heard of that boy, too. His name was Charles Dickens."

Al, you have more going for you than Dickens did when he began as a writer! You know that God is with you, call on Him, use Him as a resource, and take time to listen to His direction. And above all never give up...with His help you can do it!

Keep your dream in front of you!

Sincerely B.B. ☺

CONTENTS

X

Foreword

Things haven't changed much over the last forty years but seem to have only repeated as Alvin S. Woods shows in his book <u>Guns, Drugs, Gangs, and Anger</u>. Born and raised in the city of Detroit, Michigan, Mr. Woods recants growing up in a world of drugs after he's entrusted to run a dope den while still attending high school. His whole world changes though after getting caught carrying a pistol in an effort to show off to his buddies. That's when the drama begins for this young man who had an upbringing in a home with all the good family values. Little did he know, his irresponsibility as nothing more than a young would follow him the rest of his life, like with most of our young gangsters repeating this story day after day.

This author fills a niche in books needed that tell the truthful side to the streets not routinely taught in most homes and schools. His experience intertwines a great story with solutions helpful in teaching a lesson to young men of today and tomorrow. And while keeping the reader entertained from the first page, he explains how the drug trade became so popular to those today. He describes growing up in urban Detroit in the early seventies during a time when heroin infused the Black neighborhoods of the ghetto, only a few miles from where I also stomped the grounds, twenty years earlier. It is a must read for any young man (and old ones too) living in an urban environment where influenced by guns, drugs, or gangs. While many young men have grown into thinking they will prosper making fast cash in the streets, he shows the truth to that as he recalls what it's like being shot in an attempted robbery set up by a friend that left him clinging to his life.

In bringing the science of anger into the picture Mr. Woods gives a different reasoning to much of the crime experienced on a daily basis. Using himself as an example he shows the common factors behind much of the gun violence that goes on today. Not only being a victim, he reveals shooting a member of his own brotherhood in a rage of fury and coming close to shooting others when the temper takes over.

This book is a mirror for the young man to see himself and his outcomes in advance. This is a one of a kind memoir in the fact that not only is it a great story, it finishes with answers, diverse perspectives, and explanations to the gun and anger problems he now classifies a disease. And not left un-addressed, homicide statistics in the African American neighborhoods are also compared to that of other races and ethnicities.

There is no question a book like this is long overdue. Not only is it needed in urban neighborhoods, but all neighborhoods. The wisdom here is a teaching tool and can save some lives before lost. Guns, Drug, Gangs, and Anger gives the young man a different way to look at and address issues and responsibility dealing with drugs and violence that is taking his own life long before gets the chance to see middle age. This memoir is one to be relevant for quite some time and well utilized by those who continue to believe success and prosperity can be found on urban streets.

Dr. John Telford, Superintendent (interim)
Detroit Public Schools, September 2012

Preface

In the sixties civil rights demonstrations led by the Black Panthers, Dr. Martin Luther King Jr., and others who lost their lives in the name of democracy and fairness were common. During this time came a plan we were blind to, a plan to stifle the protestor as well as their generations of descendants to come; a plan of secret retaliation by using opiate narcotics to silence those seeking the true freedom sought through civil rights protesting.

By the early seventies, heroin flourished the neighborhoods of the protestors that started riots in a few cities like Los Angeles and Detroit. With Detroit being a Mecca to many Black folk that came from the south for jobs, it was a place with a concentration of Black families and a prime target. At the time some saw the drugs as an opportunity to make money while getting high and forgetting their troubles at the same time. Little did anyone realize, the plan we knew nothing about was to destroy the Black family at the same time of removing the Black man from his home through incarceration and death in the drug trade once we started killing each other for the profits.

While many began making small and large amounts of money from drugs came the need for guns to protect the profits. Prior to then guns were generally last resorts because everyone knew how to fight or settle disputes with mouth and mind. Guns became a tool along side of the drugs once the money needed the guard; the more drugs, the more guns. It wasn't until those seventies when we began turning on each other in the name of a quick dollar. When Black folk began making thousands of dollars the murders started and hasn't stopped since.

The purpose of this book is to bring awareness to the young man today that makes his living in the streets, or just live in urban settings. While many have inherited the dream of many from forty years ago, the reality is that there is no future in the streets with guns and drugs. Though there are those who think they are so smart they will get where none of us have made it and kept it, they may see their future in this book before living out the adventure.

There are many who only live for today, never giving thought to how it's going to be forty or fifty years later, if they live. This book gives them the opportunity to look into the real unending life of the hustler and the felon who becomes ostracized after obtaining the negative stigma.

Most importantly, this book shows the outcome of those who use intelligence and manhood to find a way of settling disputes as opposed of using guns. What is shown here is that those we feud with would actually be our best friends, but in many cases we wind up killing them before they have the chance to come to our rescue.

POP POP!

POP POP! That's all I heard
Silence fell, not a sound or word
Two guns, one chrome, one black
My daddy lying' on his back

The three of us went out of town
Thought we was just having' fun
Sis' and me hadn't the slightest idea
He went there to buy a gun

Shoes still on, feet pointed west
Blood running through a hole in his chest
Tears in her eyes, and a gun in her hand
Mama hated to shoot her man

Drunken rages, mistreating his wife
That's how daddy lost his life
His last few breaths, eyes open wide
The darkest gun lay by his side

Didn't know what it meant to die and go to heaven
At that time I was only seven

Two women in the house and me
Took to the streets running' free
Mama worked hard to keep clothes on our backs
But I was too young to know how to act

Meeting new friends, finding new hope
Finished school while slinging' dope
Went to collect money owed to me
The guy didn't pay, so I shot his TV

Needed a gun to protect myself
Needed a gun stuck in my waist
Needed a gun to gain the respect I sought
But by eighteen I'd caught my first case

POP POP! Things turned around
This time I was the one lying' down
Dudes came through to rip off my sack
Left me dying with a hole in my back

Years later I made a change in life
Started a new business and took a wife
Still kept rolling' to support my family
Got ripped off again, by somebody close to me

POP POP! Again and again
Standing in a crowd
Everybody got shot except me
But it left me crying out loud

It may be true what they say "like father like son"
And "the apple don't fall far from the tree"
But when I looked in the mirror I saw my dad,
Looking out the mirror at me

Fifty years have come and gone
Since my dad was laid in his grave
Sometimes I visit the cemetery
To give him a bath and a shave

What I miss the most in life
Is the relationship dad and I could have had
But all that never happened
Cause he was trying to go for bad

Mom always told me dad was really a good man inside
I know we could've had a lot of fun
But just as his life was ruined, so was mine
And it all started with a punk-ass gun

CHAPTER 1: JUST FOR FUN

It was around 8 p.m. For a Friday business was slow at the house I had been entrusted to run. It was payday and with a pocket full of greenbacks I decided to close down and go hang out with some of my homies. Since some of them used the diluted form of heroin some called 'scag,' I figured I'd take some and kick it with them awhile.

Selling dope was my part-time business. I was working for a couple out of New York who had set up shop in the urban environs of Detroit. I put about six or seven aluminum packets, each containing a half of a teaspoon of the powder, in a clear plastic bottle with a white cap that had a piece of tape with $3.00 written on it. It was what we sometimes used for containing the packages in the spot we sold from. I dropped the bottle in the pocket of the black full-length pea coat I was going to wear so it wouldn't be forgotten.

I had powered my nose with a few lines then put up all the paraphernalia lying around and slipped into my coat. The thought came to mind of packing the .38 just to show off my newfound lieutenant status of the neighborhood dope man. Normally I wouldn't have tried to impress friends or anyone else by taking the gun that protected the profits of the business, but my bosses had made a run to upstate New York for the weekend to take care of some dealings and left me running things. I took off the coat.

Now and then we used a shoulder holster when working in the apartment to make sure it was at hand's reach at all times. I put it on, snuggled the gun in the holster, and put my coat back on. After closing the warm wool pea coat and buttoning it, a slight bulge still protruded from behind the lapel, but it wouldn't be noticed as much with the coat unbuttoned. The concealed straps of the shoulder holster allowed me to go unnoticed with it open unless someone was looking that close, like the police, but I was only going a couple of block away and chances of running into them were slim. Though only eighteen, there was a lot of responsibility in my lap, and I was into my second year doing it.

I locked the apartment, walked to the elevator and pushed the button for my ride down two floors. After waiting a few moments, the light from the elevator seen through the translucent door windows appeared like a sun rising up from the second floor below me. I entered and pushed the first floor button. The motor of the winch cranked up, lowering me. As the elevator was about to make its stop at the first level shadows darkened the glass. After I opened the scissor like gates and then the glass doors, it was too late to close them back. Three plain-clothes detectives stood in front of me. My heart pounding, I attempted to pass through them, shunning eye contact. Taking a step to walk past, one cop noticed the bulge in my coat. He stopped me and began patting my left side, feeling the solid parcel underneath. My plans quickly changed. I wasn't about to brag and boast around my boys; I was on my way to jail.

They immediately handcuffed me and put me in the car with the driver who had remained behind the wheel when they entered the building. I remembered the bottle of dope that was in my coat pocket. *DAMN! They didn't search me thoroughly before putting me in the car. But if they find these packages of heroin in my pocket that gun will be the appetizer!* With handcuffs on it was virtually impossible to get my hands in my coat pocket without the driver noticing. A cold clammy sweat soaked me. The more I tried to move my handcuffed arms the more I sweat. Any little sound made by the squeaky leather seats would draw attention from the cop behind the wheel. I knew I couldn't be caught with that *'dog food';* my life would be ruined for sure. I had no time to panic. At any minute the cops who went into the building would be coming back.

With nothing less of a struggle I was able to feel the opening of my pocket with my right hand, yet reaching my fingers down in the deep gorge made the task like reaching for keys in a sewer. More desperate by the second, the tension of the handcuffs caused them to start cutting into the flesh of my wrist. The more the second hand advanced on the clock on the dashboard, the more I was about to piss myself. My heart beat faster and faster as I kept reaching to get my right hand into the pocket. Every ten seconds the driver would look in the rear view mirror, his eyes sometime meeting mine.

Once literally raising my body and pulling the coat pocket towards my hands, my fingers could feel the cap on the bottle. Knowing the officers would soon be walking out the door that we sat in front of, with all my might I reached hard, managing to get a few fingers around the top. Pulling the container into my hand, the closeness of the pocket sides brushed it out of my finger's clutch, allowing it to fall back down in the bottomless pouch. With a dope case haunting me I made a Herculean effort until I got my fingers on it and got it into a tight fist. Now I had to make sure the loose fitting top didn't come off and leave the contents in my pocket that would never be reached.

Pulling my hand out of my pocket, relieving the strain on my left arm, I got the bottle out with the top still intact. Now the task was to get rid of it. I couldn't drop it on the floor or leave it on the seat because they would know it was mine whether they found it on me or not. The only thing to do was stuff it through the seats. As I tried to push the bottle through the leather seats they began to squeak, and the driver once again glanced at me in his mirror. Looking for the three figures to walk out the door any second, I removed the top off the bottle and began stuffing the packs through the cracks in the seat with my fingers. The problem was, not seeing if some of the contraband got caught in the folds of my thick wool coat. Not being able to see if I pushed them all through the seats. Leaving just one of them on the seat would lead to them taking the whole seat out, finding the rest of the packages, all matching the one found.

Pushing what I thought was the last of the aluminum wrapped packages through the bench style seating, the shadows of the officers walking down the brightly lit vestibule staircases were appearing through the glass entry door of the building. Praying everything was dumped; the first cop came out the door. Still having the plastic bottle in my hand, with no place to put it left me in another struggle to put it back in my pocket with only three seconds to do it. When the light came on from the officer riding shotgun opening the door, now in a full sweat, the empty container had been pushed back into its place. It seemed I'd successfully got rid of my contraband but I wouldn't know for sure until we reached the police station and I exited the car.

After a short five-minute ride we drove into the parking lot of Detroit's 10th precinct on Elmhurst and Livernois. The large overhead garage door opened and the plainclothes detectives, a.k.a., the Big Four, drove straight into the single story brick structure. Just as the notable team of heavyweight lawmen opened all the doors at the same time like they did on the street, the adrenaline rush kicked in. It was time to find out if I left any dope on the seat of the car. The dicks moved out, taking me out with them. Looking down at the seat on my egress, I didn't see anything. They had the gun and that was enough.

Once we got into the station the questioning began with the routine humiliation. The investigators began shaking me down, fishing through all my pockets, sitting the contents of my belongings on the counter in front of me. Out came my small bankroll and change, wallet, lighter and cigarettes, and finally the bottle with $3.00 written on the top.

"What's this?" the officer asked then removed it.

"Nothing! It's just a bottle. I keep my change in it!"

I replied, drawing a smug look of doubt on the cop's face.

With a persnickety smile and unspoken words, *Yeah ok, whatever!*

Whether he suspected me of having something like drugs in the bottle or not, he had no evidence. He didn't even see the powder residue inside. I just hoped two and two wouldn't lead him to the back seat of that squad car again.

With the gun in their possession, they thought it would be amusing to let me continue to wear the empty shoulder holster. Now, the officers reporting into the station shared in a night of laughter, doing a double take when they first saw me. I was old enough to be arrested and charged with a major crime, and too young to be a cop. Though not the type to commit a crime using a gun, carrying it was committing crime enough.

I was taken into a cold fluorescent-lit room to be fingerprinted. I had never been in trouble before but I had seen people mugged and printed on television. I hadn't even been in handcuffs. The booking officer reeled an ink roller onto an inkpad then gently sloped it on a thick, worn piece of thick clear glass that had seen better days.

The officer laid a fingerprint card with my name on a device and locked it into place, exposing marked-off boxes indicating which finger was to be placed where. As he took hold of my hand and rolled the first finger in the black ink, the moment became dreamlike. Earlier that night I never thought

I'd be spending my first night in a precinct jail. I had been taught how to avoid the police, not wind up in their custody. Now all would be able to know my identity forever by the imprints of my fingers. Soon I could be classified a felon, someone that people don't trust, and most employers won't consider. I would have given anything to put things in rewind. There was no real basis for carrying a gun in the first place. Showing off had been my motivation, and a serious error of judgment. Now, the task was informing my bosses in New York, and advising my mother of my stupidity, begging for their help to get me out of the situation. Though I had been taking care of myself for a while, the reality of not getting out of this one was beyond certainty.

When the officer finished his fingerprinting he placed me in a holding cell. Because it was Friday, spending the weekend locked up until the court reconvened on Monday when I could get a bond, seemed more than likely.

The cell that had become my temporary home reeked of stale smoke, urine and alcohol, a stench that made the bullpen smell like a boarding house that roomed drunks. While only a few cigarette butts littered the floor, more noticeable were the many names, renderings and cuss-words carved into the walls by other prisoners in weak or frustrated moments. The only thing available to sit on other than a toilet was the slab of wood that they called the bed.

Sitting on my folded coat to pad my bony butt I began thinking about my fate. My mother didn't raise no jailbirds. Catching a case would place me with only one or two in the whole entire generation that had been in trouble with the law. I grew up in the church and had completed two years of confirmation into my faith by age thirteen. My dad passed when I was seven leaving me with no direction or guidance. I had done pretty well until now. Yet, still completing my education, I had already put myself on the other side of the fence. Not happy to be sitting there charged with a gun case, my agony would be worse, thinking about where I'd be if they found the few grams of heroin I dumped in their car.

* * *

With a year to go in trade school I still needed an additional year in high school to get my diploma. My mother, who we called Nan, begged me to finish school. She knew my age would be a deterrent; because of failing the eighth grade twice I would be almost twenty before finishing. I had already made up my mind though to graduate because it meant so much to her. My sister and father had done the same, as well as her. All of my extended relatives were graduates and degreed professionals. Whatever I would do, finishing school was definite.

Growing up hustling pop bottles and newspapers, the money made as a part time doorman at the dope house was more than I'd ever seen. Most of the time, on Fridays, the money remained in my pocket from payday the week before. I had even saved a few bucks, something never done before. My bosses, Norman and Bert, trusted me enough to run the business and had gotten another apartment around the corner on Boston Street to live in. Able to afford a place away from the activity, they outgrew the small apartment that was now primarily used for drug transactions and had become my new home away from home. I stayed there more than with Nan. While in school they worked the place and I worked it when they weren't there.

This was my first opportunity to run a business that had rules. Not following them could cost my life and I wasn't taking any chances. The main rule was that nobody ever went to answer the door without having a pistol in hand. Another established rule was that all the clientele had to call before they came. When a few pushed their luck while Norman was there, if he opened the door they got cussed out, including his cousin who was a cop. They didn't get in on my watch.

This was the first time I operated a business where a gun was a tool like a lathe and a hone. I learned my job quick, but in the first days I, too, got cussed out for answering the door without the pistol. It was a rule nobody broke, not even his woman. While she played more of a hands-off role, every now and then she would open the door and wait on regulars. Until now, there were two guns in the house, a relic P-38, and a five shot .38 Charter Arms snub nose. We always used the .38 when we opened the door. Now, with my inane decision, the police had it.

CHAPTER 2: DOG FOOD

It was late 1971; the flow of heroin and cocaine was increasing in the ghettos as well as it did in Detroit, and more so. The number of Cadillac Eldorados and Fleetwoods sporting wide gangster whitewalls and TV antennas were seen on any street, and parked in front of low income apartment buildings. It was all about the "Diamond in the back, sunroof top, diggin' the scene with a gangster lean." For anyone who desired to make large amounts of money, drugs were becoming the way to make it happen. With the plan quickly backfiring on the majority, those who set out to make fast money wound up addicted to the drugs they sold. It seemed like President Nixon, who then was still fresh in his tenure, turned his back on us just enough, allowing us a chance to fulfill our dreams. He was busy doing his thing while we were busy doing ours.

Over the next few years to come, many of us would make more money than our hard-working parents had seen in a lifetime, including their pensions. Hundreds of thousands of dollars were at hand to those who didn't have as much as a high-school education. Many of the customers and dealers were Vietnam vets void of education the government promised, kicked back into society with nothing else to turn to but drugs; some made millions and carelessly lost it. We were beginning to make so much money in the 'hood, police were bought, but some of the cops found more pleasure in the easy pickings – ripping us off and increasing their paychecks. Some cops even used heroin themselves, like Norman's cousin, Joe.

Those who had the best connections made the most money. They purchased their drugs in larger amounts, bought and sold it cheaper, creating more tax-free revenue. The old-heads in the 'hood set up shops from which to deal the well sought powder. Many of them were ex-pimps and owners of after-hour joints, forced to change with the times after the riot of '67 destroyed all the hoe strips. Some turned their best moneymakers into addicts and secondary dealers.

Before starting their entrepreneurships, most of the dealers were non-users of hard drugs and eventually got hooked, creating habits that led to them being their own best customers. Very few '*rolled*' that didn't wind up using the drugs they sold. The majority eventually dealt in order to support their habits. Once they began to use as much as they sold they fell in the hole, losing their customers and connections from indebtedness. Their purchases became smaller and smaller, cutting the dope so much they wound up losing all their business.

After many realized they had accumulated enormous habits, they checked into methadone clinics to get free medication. All that turned out to be was a legitimate way of controlling drugs and keeping up with people and the names of those in the city were addicts. For me it was another way of making money until they made us take the pills in front of them. While we had the chance, we sold them to other users in the 'hood who couldn't afford the real thing.

The focus on drugs became so intent many forgot about their families and the importance of them. Dealers were catching cases and finding themselves in jail, cut out of the lives of their wives and children. Addiction became as common as the drug itself. Some found the upkeep of their habits more important than a place to live. The late Dr. King's dream seemed overshadowed with darkness and unquestionably more difficult to bring into reality while those responsible for making the change were in another world. It appeared that all the lives lost in the prior decade were in vain.

As the addictions became more intense in the already poor neighborhoods, the importance of family and children developed into second-hand concerns. Marriage, breast-feeding our infants, and building families, learned from our ancestry, lost importance. As with many, heroin became my blanket and moneymaker. I was into the life everyone dreamed of – a trance inspired by the character "Goldie" in the movie "*Superfly.*" At the time, it seemed like everyone who watched the movie believed selling drugs would be the way out of poverty. Many people lost their lives or put them on the line for the quick dollar. Most of the survivors no longer have a penny of the money they made. Many would die in their dreams at an early age.

My pursuit and charisma had me in with the biggest dope-dealers in the neighborhood. I was still in school while running one of the most sought-after dope houses on my side of town because of the quality product. In a matter of time I drove Cadillacs to school instead of riding buses. Norman traded in his DeVille (that he had when I met him by fixing it after meeting him through a friend old enough to buy from him), for a slightly used Fleetwood Brougham. And when driving it to school one day my counselor ran the tags and came to me with the information showing me the name on the registration, which was registered to Bert. He seemed suspicious because it was the second Cadillac I'd driven to school. He knew I was probably connected with drugs or something. It didn't matter to me though cause I was doing what I thought was cool. I just didn't know where it would lead me like he did.

CHAPTER 3: JAIL HOUSE CRAP GAME

After being transferred downtown next morning to the Wayne County Jail, I was moved several times before getting a cell to myself. First in a bullpen with those who had auras of everything I wasn't, including thieves, stickup men, and those you would have to be a fool to trust with a five-dollar bill. After being fed with the usual jailhouse sandwich and a pint of milk I was led to my first cell. It was on a quiet block with only about ten of the twenty or so cells filled. Cell numbers identified everybody and became a name; mine was seven. While not superstitious, the number didn't fit the bad luck experienced. Though no cell numbers in a jail cell were an indication of good luck, the cellblock was much quieter than noisy ones that could be heard in the sections we passed on the floor.

Unlike the cell in the precinct, this one had a mattress that padded the distance between the cold hard steel and my slender 145-pound frame. Sitting on the thin green mattress to myself, *Damn, I'm supposed to be at the apartment running the business and here I am sitting in jail without a bond. I don't want to call Norman. The only person to call is Nan and if I don't call her I'll have to sit here until Tuesday because Norman and Bert won't get back 'til late Monday.*

The solitude gave me the first chance to feel the pain of losing my best friend, Theodore, only a few months prior. Losing him was like losing a parent or a sibling. We were tight like toes in a shoe. We knew all the same people and did the same things. His death left me stupefied; we were friends since before I started running the streets and hanging out. He died after getting stabbed in the heart when making the trip to get a dime bag of weed. We went to the same school until my getting kicked out of junior high and being sent to trade school. He lived directly behind me and we'd been friends since we were kids. All left to remember him was a picture that Norman took when Theodore and me went to a party at Norman's, which is when I was introduced to the old-head. When Theodore died, Norman told me he would be my best friend and gave me the picture he had taken of us at the party. Consciously knowing it was a terrible idea for a dope man to be my best friend, he was the only other person I now saw as much as Theodore. Friendship wasn't what I was seeking from the dope man; it was the money, something that had captivated my interest like it did everyone else during that era.

Before lunch, the guard had called out half of the guys on the cellblock who made bail or were moved. I called for the warden to let me make my phone call I'd been promised. Not needing money, but to make a collect call left me feeling uncomfortable. While I wasn't expecting her to refuse the call, the thought of an operator calling her was distressing. Nan, never the fussing type, listened to my solicitation for a possible favor if I wasn't able to get out of the predicament I'd gotten myself in. She was always a strong woman irrespective to her 125-pound frame. Though she didn't have a lot of money, she had means to get or do whatever she wanted. I figured cash alone would be able to get me out and that could be gotten from Norman when he returned on Monday. Her main concern was that I was all right. She probably wasn't surprised though because she knew I was on the wrong track and had been so for years. I didn't ever think I'd wind up in jail, but probably wind up dying with my shoes on like my dad.

Only talking a short time because the call would run up her bill, I bid her goodbye and told her not to worry about me and that I would be fine. I returned to the cellblock to take a midday snooze, but the heroin in my system having worn off, left me feeling like a naked man with the chill of winter that penetrated the jailhouse windows. Though I didn't use dope every day at the time, I used it enough to have the urge to make me want it. Instead of sleeping sound, I only slept half the time in comfort.

With nothing else to do in my cell other than look through the bars that stood between freedom, and me I smoked one of the cigarettes out of the remaining half pack I had left and went to sleep.

No sooner had I dozed off, the turnkey came to the head of the block and called names; mine was one. *I know nobody is bailing me out! Wonder what's up?*

"You all are going to be moved to another cell. We're transferring you because there are only a few of you in here," the turnkey told those of us left. I hated to hear it because my cell had gotten comfortable not having to continuously talk to a bunch of people identifying myself by a compartment number and crime. The silence was what I had always been accustomed to - no drama, no arguments, and no problems.

"Woods! Come with me; you'll be moved upstairs!"

After a few minutes of walking and taking an elevator with the prison warden, I followed him to one of the loud blocks like the ones I heard when entering the dungeon. I was placed in my quarters, having to walk through the inmates on the catwalk in order to get to my new cell, number thirteen. That's right, with all the floors with jail cells numbered thirteen, I wound up with one.

The block was full of prisoners. Speaking with hesitation and not pretending to be hard, I carried the mattress and my belongings through the crowd to my cell. Half of them were on the walk, talking, and the other half stayed in their steel and concrete compartments. I went inside my new temporary encased loss of freedom, figuring returning back out on the walk would be a good idea since walking through everyone on my way in. If anyone thought me to be a bit bourgeois it could result in unneeded trouble.

The guys on the concourse seemed to accept my invasion into their privacy without the display of capitulation, leading them to think that I may be prey for the day. After completing my introductions and lying like everyone else about what got them there I went to my cell. Though talking may have been an escape and a time killer, I wasn't in the mood for socializing. The thought on my mind was being back home and serving the loyal customers that made for my payday, enjoying my freedom and lack of restrictions.

During the run of the day, after becoming restless, I left my cell and talked to some of the guys who weren't asleep in their bunks. Those who weren't there for moving violations were there mostly for felonious assaults, larceny, and domestic abuse. What everybody had most in common was a need for a cigarette. The few in my pack wouldn't supply everyone who wanted one so mine were saved for when in my cell. The more we talked, the more I realized this wasn't a place to see again. It was my first time getting the chance to interact with those whose conversations confirmed getting locked up was a regular routine. Finding it more of a pleasure, my cell became my domain. I slept for most of the evening and all night.

The curtain of windows directly in front of my cell gave way to the shining sunbeams that Sunday morning. I forced myself to sleep most of the night, tossing and turning from the uncomfortable bunk. Steel walls and bars encompassed me. The inmates in the cell were already yelling out.

"Turn-key, Turn-key!"

Everyone among the ten or so on the block seemed to have some reason to call. I had a reason to call for him too, but it was too early to call Nan, so I sat there until breakfast came a few moments later. The bars on the cell doors opened, giving us freedom to the catwalk. The trustee came moments later with breakfast. Everyone patiently waited for the trustee to walk half the distance of the catwalk that separated us from him by bars. He pushed his cart down the outskirts of the walk carrying donuts, cereal, milk, and coffee, serving it through the bars. I had to walk a short distance where he stopped to serve. I waited in line and got my grub. After making a few steps toward my cell, a confrontation could be heard. One of the inmates began running from the trustee who had picked up the large container of hot coffee, chasing him. Knowing he couldn't hit the inmate, he threw the scalding contents through the bars at him, but at that moment the guy running was next to me. Before I was able to move, the guy collided with me, knocking my coffee out my hand and the hot coffee the orderly threw came in my direction like from an elephant's trunk. The guy he was throwing the coffee at had apparently intimidated the trustee and didn't get hit at all, but I was on fire.

Standing in hysterics, wanting to call for the turnkey to bite his nose off, I was more shocked than angry. The jailhouse flunkey immediately apologized. I couldn't be mad because he wasn't trying to hit me. Though now wet in a cold can, I made it back to my cell with a handful of donuts, milk, and cereal in acceptance for the slip-up. Half-wet and smelling like coffee, I took the extra grub and went back to my cell, without my cup of java that had already started drying on the floor.

When lunch came I still had snacks from breakfast. Paying for his mistake, the apologetic fellow brought me an armful of lunch. He gave me apples, sandwiches, chocolate milk, white milk, and twice as much as what was on the menu. The five-course eat left me ready for a midday siesta.

Dried out by the time dinner came, a different trustee than the one that scalded me served the supper. I still had food left from lunch but that was what I'd have when getting hungry after the lights went out.

All things being relative the dinner of chicken potpie was like one of the steaks they served a few blocks away at the Flaming Embers Steakhouse on Woodward and Grand Circus Park. I ate the lukewarm jailhouse delicacy, snacked on some of my stash and lay down, anticipating a positive outcome in court the following day.

The next morning I appeared before the judge. He set a bond of five thousand dollars with a surety. Five hundred dollars in cash was needed and a guarantee for the rest of the money in security, meaning Nan would have to put her house up in order to bail me out. After the short appearance, I was placed back in the bullpen with angry and remorseless criminals awaiting their fate. Waiting more than a couple of hours, I was hungry from missing lunch and given a sandwich while waiting to be shipped a block away back to the county lockup. Once there, I was taken to a new cellblock, which was full. They gave me another mattress and took me to cell number eleven. The significance of the numbers that identified me left me feeling tossed like in a craps game.

Feeling dumb was an understatement with the thought of having to ask Nan for help, knowing I was adding strain to someone who was struggling, as most without the added income of a husband, who are forced to make a living as a domestic. Nevertheless, she had the only means available for me to escape the mess I'd gotten in. Many things passed through my mind but the thing crossing it most was the predicament I was putting other people in.

The dream of having my own cell was once inconceivable but now became something I wished for.

No sooner than moving into the cell, problems began that afternoon. Before getting comfortable I received a request from one of the guys in the block, a guy who they called "Frog."

"Hey number eleven!" he called out.

"What!" I answered.

"Hey, man! I want your donuts in the morning!"

Not knowing what he looked like or the look he carried on his face when he made the statement, my idea of handling the situation took me back to junior high.

"Yeah ok!" I replied, knowing this was an indication of trouble, and before it was over I'd more than likely be the one winding up on the floor.

The only time prisoners were able to stroll the catwalk was after the gates were opened at about seven a.m. While taking him seriously, giving in to that type of demand was unheard of in my world. I grew up in a school system where there were fights every day and I had to fight too. I had my ass whipped before and handed out a few. Without a gun or a shim, he was still going to catch the first punch regardless of his size. Though I'd been arrested and placed in a jail cell, I was still "top dawg" in my 'hood and also in my mind. He wasn't about to get shit. What he didn't realize is that his method of intimidation pissed me off.

"Fuck him!"

The gates opened the next day.

The trustees served breakfast. Just as "Frog" had predicted, donuts, coffee, and milk were on the menu. Hungry like most, I ate my white powdered donuts and washed them down with the milk. I lay back on my bunk and began to think about how they were going to approach me.

No sooner than I relaxed I got a yell from Frog.

"Hey number eleven, you got them donuts?"

"Naw!" I replied.

"What happened to them?" he asked.

"I ate them!" *What the fuck you thought?*
In my mind I knew problems were about to arise from me not giving up my donuts. If I had given in, there's no telling how high the ceiling would have been. Once giving in, I'd be under someone else's control. He wasn't about to get my donuts or the milk, or anything I had. I continued to lay on my bunk in hopes there actually wouldn't be any trouble, but was waiting for it.

It got a little quiet after his call for the donuts. I figured if we would lock horns it would be on the catwalk. He didn't come to my cell and I wasn't actually going to look for trouble.

A couple of hours passed. Just as I began to doze a shadow appeared in front of the light coming from outside the cell. Frog had arrived with one of his boys. He was four or five inches taller and about fifty pounds heavier. I never thought I'd have to fight two people and could see myself about to get my ass kicked. As Frog crossed the threshold into my cell I threw the first punch at his face, knowing it might be my best one.

Seeming to be unaffected by my blow, both Frog and his boy jumped me. Trying to fight back, the two overpowered me. The only thing I could do was cover my head and face. The two of them beat the hell out of me for almost five minutes. It seemed they hammered me for days. The last thing I remember was getting up and passing out on my bunk.

When becoming conscious, what seemed like hours later, I'd been hurt pretty bad. My head felt like it had been beaten to a pulp. The only thing I knew to do was call for the turnkey to let me out to seek medical assistance. I staggered to the entrance of the block and called for the turnkey. Once the guard came and saw me, he didn't have to ask any questions. He immediately took me off the block to get help, and took me to the infirmary to get treatment. Not having seen myself in the mirror, I learned from the doctor my face was bruised quite badly. One eye was nearly closed and my whole head ached. From the way everyone was looking at me I knew I'd gotten it bad. Nevertheless I held on to my pride and dignity.

I stayed in the sickbay the rest of the day and called Norman after he made it home that evening, informing him of my predicament. He called Nan and they made arrangements to bail me out. She agreed to put up the collateral, and my employers put up the five hundred dollars cash.

When allowed to see me, both Norm and Bert had a look of awe on their face when they saw mine. I had actually been beaten so bad they hardly recognized me and could tell from the look on their faces the pain I was suffering was less than the damage done to my head. When getting the chance to see the damage myself, I could hardly recognize my own face from the lopsidedness of my head and facial features. I was a poster child for the cliché being "beaten so bad my own mother wouldn't know me."

I made bail before going into another cell.

* * *

By the time I went to court all the bruises and unevenness of my head had healed. I received a year of probation with the assistance of my mother's attorney. I never trusted him though because he appeared to be too friendly to the judge and it seemed like he would have done a better job by speaking up more for me. Still in school at the time and never having been in trouble, I felt that if I'd been some rich kid I never would have spent the night in jail on day one. The lawyer seemed to place his interest in getting closer to the judge more than winning my case. But for the meantime, I was out of trouble.

At least I thought.

CHAPTER 4: A GUN OF MY OWN

Norman managed to get another gun to replace the one lost to the cops. He was lucky enough to get another one just like the one I lost, only newer. He also bought a .22 cal. pistol made on a .357 frame. That one was mine to use while working. The gun was so large it should have scared anyone out of taking the chance getting shot by it. Though we didn't operate a dangerous business because of the well-known clientele, we didn't want to be seen as an easy target by someone setting us up.

Being linked to the neighborhood dope man made things easy to acquire. Once the customers got comfortable with me waiting on them instead of Norman, they began to let me know of any deals on goods that came their way. I could get anything for drugs. One of them asked me if I was interested in buying a .38 he had. He told me he only wanted a hundred dollars for it and it was like brand new.

"Bring it to me and if it looks good I'll buy it!" I told him.

When the customer came back with the unloaded gun for me to see, he had it in a Crown Royal bag with the yellow drawstring. He opened it and pulled out the most beautiful stainless steel Smith & Wesson .38 that had a four-inch barrel. It really was like new. The smell from the barrel couldn't trace a scent of gunpowder. It looked like it had never been fired. Without hesitation I hurried and gave him the hundred dollars he asked for with a smile. I had a piece of my own that was better than all three of the guns Norman had there in the apartment.

I graduated from trade school in that summer of '72, but still had one more year to cross the finish line. My debt from skipping school and being a clown in intermediate school was almost paid. After losing a whole year in school by failing twice, I found myself in the eleventh grade without a possibility of graduating until damn near twenty years old.

While being in my new high school, Chadsey, I found myself in the company of total strangers. The main thing different was that after spending almost three years in an all-boys vocational school, I also found myself in the company of many young ladies. While my focus should have been more on them, my vision was making money. Besides, I had as many dollars as needed and enough game to get any young lady wanted. Running after them just wasn't my way, and most of the time I had the company of one anyway at home.

For a while, mingling with the new students wasn't my thing either. I was there on business, which was to finish about six classes in a one-year period. My schedules were cinches, the first of two semesters taking four classes and the last two in summer school. Taking all six in one term would have been the preferred method, but I needed three math classes and could only take two at a time.

My schedule forced me to be one of the last ones in school every day and the first one out. The main person I took to first was a guy who drove a new Mercury Marquis. The ride was sharp as the women he drove to and from school. They called him *"Proc,"* short for Proctor. He was the only one other than myself driving cars to school every day that were almost new. It was 1972, and I drove a '71 Monte Carlo on most days and my boss's new triple red Cadillac Fleetwood occasionally. It would have been obvious to someone looking from the outside in that I was on the wrong track, but a total stranger, nobody questioned me.

Feeling I was a bad influence, I distanced myself from those I should have been making my friends. I was selling heroin to people with habits and couldn't see mixing the students up in my kind of business. I was the guy that momma always warned her daughter to stay away from.

I couldn't blame her.

Because 'Proc' and me both drove late model cars with flash we had some commonality. Anyone in high-school driving new cars has always been a hit. So when we parked together eyes focused on us. Meeting only a few people, my distance was kept. After months passed, learning Proc had a liking for the *dog food* I was dealing I made the decision to take him on as a client.

Though it was a rule not to let everybody know my business, I eventually broke it, turning my friend on to something I knew he would like. The people I worked for had a reputation for keeping a better product than commonly found. The place I worked from remained a secret though until after getting to know him pretty well, which was close to the end of my occupancy of hall space.

I was a totally different person at home than at school. At school I carried books. At my job I carried a gun. Waiting on people who needed drugs and taking their money was my work. My boss's clientele were mainly working people. Most users at that time had jobs and the majority were weekend users. Eventually I let Proc come and make a buy. He fit in with those coming and going because he looked a few years older than he actually was. He seemed to have a liking for the powder. He was making a buy once or twice a week by the time we graduated from school. Though he had the nice ride, his money was always wrinkled and balled – like he had hustled up on two dollars at a time. I knew it was only a matter of time before he would be running short. The only problem was that we had the kind of business that never made it a habit to give people credit for drugs because of it working against the trade; once you give credit, your customer tends not to pay. Not only have you lost a client but the money you would have made dealing with them. Nevertheless, when he eventually came short, I let him owe me. He paid me the first few times just like he said he would. Not letting his credit use become a habit, I had a cut-off point and he paid me whenever I let him owe me.

When it came near time to graduate it was also time to collect the money Proc owed me. I had managed to let him owe me about fifty dollars, which, in '73, would compare to at least two hundred in 2010. He seemed to have been hesitant about paying me, but it was my fault because of giving him more credit after he had neglected what he already owed.

For over a week or two he played possum, dodging me. When I tried calling him he couldn't be reached. Nevertheless, I wanted my money, eventually going by his house to get paid but when seeing him he claimed he didn't have my money. Usually, I wouldn't have made a big deal out of it because it was far less than what was kept in my pocket. The problem was that he seemed to be on the run, avoiding me. When finally contacting him after numerous calls he made a promise to pay me in a few days. I figured he still wouldn't have it when he said, but had to give him a chance to pay.

I was patient for as long as he had asked me to be. It was a Friday, payday, it was time to pay him a personal visit after making up my mind that if he didn't pay me he would have to give me something to insure payment. Once he let me in his house I would have collateral if he didn't have my money. I packed my new piece just in case, figuring he wasn't about to just let me walk out of his house with his goods and just stand there.

Upon reaching his house his I saw his car was parked in the driveway. I rang the doorbell of the upstairs flat he lived in. He buzzed me in.

I imagined the only reason he let me in was because I saw his car outside. He knew my purpose for being there – to collect my money.

"What up, man? You got my ends?" I asked.

I knew he wasn't ready to pay me because he hadn't called me to come and get it.

"Naw man! I ain't got 'em yet."

"I'm tired of waiting on you, man! I need my money. What you got I can hold til you get my cash? I'm tired of waiting on you!"

At that particular moment my focus was on what had a value in his house that I could pick up and walk out with. He didn't have anything other than a couple of couches and a portable TV in the two-family flat he lived in by himself.

Before giving it much thought I had picked up his portable black and white TV off the stand.

"I need my money, man," I said.

The size of his eyes grew, when he saw me picking up what looked like the only thing of value in the house.

"What you doin' with my TV?"

"I'm takin' this 'til you pay me my money!" I said, snatching the plug out of the wall by the cord.

"Naw, you can't do that, man!" he cried.

"Bullshit! I've been waiting on you too long, man! I'm takin' this 'til you pay me."

He reached to take back what looked like his only possession. As he tugged to take it back from me I pulled my .38. Even though he saw me pull my piece his mission was not to let me leave with his television. As he used all the energy he had to regain it, I cocked the hammer on my gun, aiming the barrel at the screen, pulled the trigger and watched the tube explode into a million pieces. He was left holding the frame in his hand as I walked out of his flat and got into my car and left.

On my way home, I realized my ambition to use a gun was fueled by my temper and resistance to be played. Proc probably didn't figure I would go to such drastic moves to get my money, but figuring he had it at some point and just didn't give it to me. I was sure if he had only what he owed me he would probably rather get high than pay his bill and also knew that upon graduating I might never see him again.

It didn't really matter much anymore if I got paid or not. I wasn't expecting him to pay me now after shooting his television set. I figured we were now even. I never returned again to collect my money. The dumbest thing about my action was that it left me in a no win situation, and no reason to demand anything, while at the same time showing a lack of wisdom – dumb.

I graduated from high school in August of '73 as planned, completing a fourteen year quest for my diploma – a prerequisite to move further in education, allowing me to go to most any college I wanted in the future. If it weren't for my mother I probably wouldn't have finished. As much as she did for me letting her down for any reason was out the question, so I stuck it out until getting my cap and gown. I felt proud to hang Chadsey's, red and yellow tassel from my car's rear view mirror sporting the shiny 1973 metallic year emblem. The only thing I didn't like about it was that it wasn't the blue and white representing Central High, the school that should have been my alma mater.

* * *

I starting dating a young lady named Arronette who was introduced to me by a friend of Deb's. She was a little over a year younger than me. At first it took me a while to take to her because we weren't drawn to each other by chemistry. I didn't have anyone else kicking it with so I began spending time with her. Though she was nice looking I couldn't see myself in a long-term relationship, but kicking it with her was better than being alone.

After coming to know her enough to trust her I took her to the apartment a few times before introducing her to Norman and Bert. We got along pretty good, getting closer to her as time went on. When Bert met her she was skeptical because she was a total stranger and Bert was always that way about everyone. She interrogated her like the police. She wasn't totally drawn to her either. While knowing her brother and figuring she was safe to have around, the unknown still encompassed her even though she had never done anything wrong or out of order. She didn't appear to have any other guys she was seeing or sneaking around with. Most of the time during weekends she was with me. Other times through the week I'd see her when picking her up for a few hours.

She turned out to be a good acquaintance. We talked on the phone during the night hours while at the apartment alone waiting for customers to straggle through. One night while we talked I got the wild idea to shoot myself in the leg to see what she'd do once hearing the gun go off, learning of me accidentally shooting myself. I wondered what it would feel like being shot with a small caliber round in the flesh. The idea was to see how long it would take for her to make it to the apartment.

It didn't take much for me to act on the thought. I was a daredevil all my life, so pulling the trigger was a cinch after giving a little thought to what could happen. Using the .38 was out of the question so I used the .22. I didn't think about the nerve damage that could have happened but did think about hitting an artery and having major bleeding. Nevertheless, those thoughts weren't enough to keep me from pulling the trigger, so I took aim at the flesh part of my leg and let the hammer fly.

Pow! The gun went off.

"What happened?" she shouted in the phone.

"I just shot myself," I said.

"I'll be right there!"

While it wasn't a true test to prove *anything* other than me being a fool, I measured her attraction by the amount of time it would take for her to get there. I was dumb in more ways than one.

While dumb enough to shoot myself, I knew not to call the EMS. The police would be the first ones to get there once calling for help. The mission was to drive myself to the hospital; that part was included in the plan once having made up my mind to do it. I sat on the couch feeling the pain from the small slug. There was no sign of blood anywhere. The bullet went straight through my leg and into the faux leather sofa I was resting on.

The night was slow. Usually the doorbell would have rung, but nobody had called. Sitting, waiting, the pain in my leg was beginning to cease. The doorbell rang about ten minutes after the foolishness. I didn't know who it could have been; Arronette didn't have enough time to make it that fast because I knew she would have had to walk, which would have taken almost thirty minutes. I spoke into the intercom.

"Who is it?" I said.

"Arronette."

Damn! How in the hell did she get here so fast?

I buzzed her in.

While she climbed the stairs to the third floor, I was preparing to leave. Only a few seconds passed before she knocked on the door. I opened it.

"Are you alright?" she questioned.

"How did you get here so fast?"

"I ran!"

I knew damn well she was lying. It would take a fast driving car at least seven or eight minutes driving through traffic lights to make it to my place from where she lived. She was also turning out to be a big liar, so it didn't matter how much she cared about me. I knew I could only go so far with someone that couldn't be trusted to tell the truth. Maybe that's what I was feeling inside.

We left the apartment and I drove to the hospital in Nan's car that I had most of the time. Upon arriving and checking myself in the doctors on staff examined me and after a few minutes the police were looking in my face.

"What happened?" they asked.

"I got shot walking down the street!" I answered.

"Where did this happen at?"

"Right around the corner from where I live."

I knew telling them it was an accident would lead to them wanting to get in the apartment to get the gun. While they had my address on my information it was to Nan's house. They wouldn't know anything about the apartment unless I told them. Their plan was to confiscate it once they found out.

"Where is that?"

"Boston and Wildemere. I was walkin' down the street and heard a gunshot. The next thing I knew I got hit in the leg!"

They knew I was lying, but had no proof of anything otherwise. Seeing it was going nowhere they didn't waste much time with me. They left almost as quick as they appeared.

When the doctors finishing their x-rays and exam, they told me there wasn't anything they could do for my leg because it was just a flesh wound. The bullet went straight through without hitting any arteries or causing any major damage. They couldn't stitch the wound so there was nothing for them to do but release me.

I went home.

After the first day my leg got real sore and stiff. The doctors gave me a set of crutches to use, which came in handy because it became difficult to walk by the third day. I still didn't know if I could trust my girl. Eventually she told me she hitched a ride to my place and didn't run after all. It was good I had more than one reason for shooting myself. Had I not wanted to know how it felt, the effort would have been wasted.

CHAPTER 5: THE SET UP

Working in the apartment was like working any job. After working all week I found it still a need to hook up with some of my friends from the 'hood. One of my friends named Willie who also hung with us from time to time wound up being one of the few friends I kept in touch with. When we were younger we both had paper routes. He had his before I got mine but he got locked down during the time we were both still delivering the papers. Back then he stayed around the corner and down the street in the next block from Theodore and another friend, Eldon, who lived between Wildemere and Dexter. We used to go collect from our customers together to add a bit of security. The worst thing about him was that he had a thing for snatching purses. He would always be asking us to participate in something I wouldn't do if paid for it and couldn't conceive the idea. But since we were always looking for something to do, the first thing to come out of his mouth was the same all the time.

"Let's get a purse! Come on let's get a purse!"

His dirty works finally caught up with him when he accosted and half stripped down a lady openly in the foyer of an apartment building, patting her butt and taking her purse. For some reason he thought he could call the lady and go visit her to have sex with her. When he went to the house and started walking up the walkway the police walked out the door and locked him up for a couple of years.

Since we had always been cool with each other when I ran into him after getting out we stayed in contact with each other and hung out sometimes, especially on weekends. He had a girlfriend named Pam and had been talking about getting married. After she began spending time with him on some of the Fridays after he got off work, I became a fifth wheel when we went somewhere together. Pam had a cousin and thought we might hit it off so she introduced us. The drawback was that she was pregnant and already had a son who was a year old. I couldn't see hooking up with a girl who already had kids because of not having any of my own. I agreed to meet her though in spite of her pre-existing family.

I met the young lady named Beverly, when Will, Pam and me went by her house. She came outside to the car where we were parked and Pam introduced us. She was about five foot three or four and gave me a much different vibration than Arronette. Her stomach was camouflaged with a loosely fitting white shirt and made it hard to tell just how pregnant she was. We talked for a few minutes before finding out she was six months older than me, but it really didn't seem to make a difference to either of us. The only negative aspect was that taking her, as my woman would be starting something that I couldn't cut-off when tiring of the relationship. Once her kids become attached to me I would be like their dad, which was something I was a little too young to take on.

We talked for almost an hour before we left. I got her phone number because she was still someone I liked talking to. She had something about her that was different than all the other young ladies I'd met. I told her I'd call and did so when I got home. Before noticing, we were on the phone a couple of hours. We shared a lot in common and she was much more street savvy than many of the ladies I knew. What I liked about her most was that she seemed to be true at heart.

Months passed and Beverly and me had become very close. During the last weeks of her pregnancy we continued to talk on the phone. We sometimes talked for hours and when I had time I'd go and see her. After she had the baby she'd come by and spend a little time with me. The apprehension about being with a woman with two kids disappeared. I had already begun accepting her son. He was only a year old and I always had a liking for kids. Now that Bev and me had made an attachment to one another what was hers was becoming mine, namely the kids.

When Bert met Beverly she took right to her. It was nothing like the skepticism she showed for Aarronette. Actually they hit it off right from the beginning. She didn't even question Bev like she did everybody else. They got along from day one and she took to her almost like a young sister. Once their relationship was approved I began letting Bev occasionally spend the night with me. Eventually she spent more time at the apartment than she did at home.

Upon telling Nan about my newfound love she didn't say much or seem to welcome the relationship. She explained to me she thought the idea of me taking on a ready-made family wasn't a good idea. After all, I didn't have any kids of my own and it may hamper the possibility of her having grandkids by me. Nevertheless, once she got to know Bev she took a liking to her just as much as I did.

* * *

By the time I'd finished school I was making more money than the average factory worker. Fridays got even better when I started working at the spot full time. Every week I got paid two hundred and fifty dollars. Norman began letting me pay myself instead of waiting for him on payday. I wasn't paying any rent or bills so all the money could be saved or spent. Since the apartment was where most of my time was spent, I bought a four-channel component system to put in my den where I slept. Norman had already started a collection of jewelry, including a diamond studded coke spoon and a huge diamond cluster ring. I also had a cluster ring made that had over a carat and a half of diamonds. Norman's cousin sold me a heavy gold nugget ring that needed a diamond set in it, but a diamond needed for that size ring would cost thousands so just put the ring in my stash.

I had access to just about anything wanted. One of my first flights on a plane was to New York to pick up a package and bring it back. The government wasn't searching people at random and there was a lot less enforcement on drug trafficking. Once it was shown I could be trusted to make the trips and bring back their stuff without stealing some of it I made even more trips. I got paid bonuses when making them and that helped to add to my stash. When the money started stacking I took several hundred dollars to give to Nan but she knew I was getting the money in ways I shouldn't have. When I offered to give her some of my pay she always refused to accept it.

"Save your money. I don't need any of it, but I'll put it up for you," she told me.

Knowing all along, I figured she probably wouldn't take it. So I just had her to put it up for me hoping that one day she would need it. She could always be trusted because she always had money though it wasn't a lot. I learned the same habit from her to always have some kind of money available.

By the time Christmas was nearing Bev and me were pretty tight. I'd become a young part-time father and her man. Our relationship moved faster than I'd expected. I really came to like her because she showed she was game and was the type that wouldn't leave her man in a fight, but fight with him. I met and came to know her father who was a really cool old dude.

He stood about 6'2" with weight in proportion. Everyone called him by the nickname "Big Daddy." Once we met it didn't take long for us to take to each other as well as me and his daughter. He soon started looking at me like his son in law. Sometimes he would come by and visit us at the apartment. He didn't know what I was doing though in the apartment. When he came around I shut all activity down. Since his daughter had started spending so much time with me, he bought her a car to make the trip back and forth and so we both had transportation. I didn't have a car of my own, only access to them whenever needed.

One day at the apartment, alone, I had a visit from a dude named Dickie who I met through my sister. I'd met him over my mother's house when he came to visit Deb. He appeared about ten years older than her and almost fifteen years older than me. I easily peeped him because like they say in the old school "Game knows game." He was into the same thing as me, selling dog food. Though he was a shifty eyed character with a pencil thin mustache and had a sinister look about him, the last thing expected of him was being a cop. After he found out I was also handling he invited me by to sample some of the product he was selling, figuring it was better than what I had. Upon seeing him snort some of the scag I figured he wouldn't have been a cop. Cops can fake it but they would never get high for a little fish like me.

I eventually trusted him enough to come by my apartment and sample my product. He learned, after sampling the powder I had access to, that it was much better than his and that I was more consistent in keeping it. He bought some for his personal use a couple of times while he waited on his supplier to get straight. He also had a hustle selling meat that he was getting hot from supermarkets. I bought a few steaks from him a couple of times. One day he came by while I had been counting my money in the back bedroom of the apartment. I'd just settled a lawsuit from an accident Theodore and me were in one night before he passed. We were hanging out in Nan's car and got rear-ended. Theodore's mother got his share of what was coming to him and I got mine, seventeen hundred dollars. I added some more to the stack of mostly small bills, which added up to around two grand. Wrapping three rubber bands around the bundle I pushed it under a pillow.

When the bell rang I buzzed him in the building. When he made it upstairs I let him in the apartment. Since trusting him a little because he was a dealer like me, I invited him to come to the back room where I packaged dope and counted money. We walked from the front door to the back of the apartment; at the same time we entered the room, both our eyes landed on the money thought pushed under the pillow. Though I attempted to rush in front of it and push it under the throw cushion, it was useless. The gleam in his eye and the stunning smile on his face expressed he had already seen too much, even though his front was of a character having more than me.

Though it could be compared to almost ten thousand today, I didn't see it as anything more than a bundle of cash. It was only some of what I had. Now, not only did he know I had drugs, he knew I had a large sum of loot as well as the diamond rings and jewelry I sometimes sported. By the next day I'd forgot about the smile on his grill, the look in his eye, and the events of that day.

The week passed. Three days after Christmas on a Friday night Dickie called me over to his house to pick up some meat like I'd done the couple of times in the past since we'd met. Bev had invited one of her girlfriends over who had a child about a year old so I shut things down for the night.

I went to Dickie's and picked up the meat he called me about. When leaving his house I went back home to the apartment. When returning to the building I was happy to see Willie and Pam outside, who had come to visit. We caught the elevator to my floor. When the elevator stopped at the third floor Will opened the door for me because my hands were filled. When stepping out, the only thing noticeable was the nose of a long barreled, nickel-plated .38 caliber revolver, which the first of two men carried.

They let Will and Pam walk on away, not knowing they came in the building with me and were my friends. If they did, their plan was already in motion and wasn't about to be cancelled.

I had no idea the visit may have saved my soon to be lost life. The stickup men didn't see my friends come into the front door of the building and get on the elevator with me. They had been waiting inside of the building and didn't see them when we all came in.

I recognized the second of the two figures who walked out of the staircase adjacent to the elevator as being a friend of Dickie's, whom I met one day while visiting. Right away I knew I'd been set up. He had a long knife in his hand. Knowing he knew me, I figured we were all definite victims for a homicide before this all ended.

Everything fell into place; like watching freeze frames flashing quickly on a movie screen. That moment I realized why my arms were full of packages; it was all part of the plan. If I *did* have a gun they knew I wouldn't be able to get to it. That was the idea behind the meat, and my stopping at the store only made their job easier by adding on even more load.

The problem was that they weren't looking for anyone to be on the elevator with me when I exited. The stick-up men didn't know who they were and that they were with me, allowing them to keep walking. The first dude grabbed hold of my collar and steered me towards my apartment with his gun stuck in my ribcage.

He ordered, "Come on! Don't try nothin'!" as the one I knew by the name Pee Wee, who had the knife, moved around the side of me.

I knew if they got in my apartment there would be dead and cut up bodies when they left. It was common knowledge of decapitated bodies being found stuffed in garbage bags all over Detroit at that time. I couldn't see myself being laid on the floor and the back of my head blown out or my body cut up, packed in a garbage bag, and lastly identified by a toe tag with my name on it.

My nerves were in shambles possibly living the last few minutes of my life. I had only a few seconds to use them as I neared the door. I had schooled Beverly on the rules routinely and made sure she understood them.

"Never open the door without having a pistol in your hand." I banked on her having it.

It would be my only way of getting us out of this shit. Whatever my move would be it would lead to me getting the gun from her when she opened the door, but I was hoping she would see what was going on when she looked through the peephole. The stickup men didn't know my plan and I wasn't positive she'd have the gun if she opened the door. All I could do was pray it was in her hand.

Stopping at the door, the one with the gun ordered,

"Open it!"

"I left my key and I've got to knock for my lady to open it!" I lied.

Not having time to figure whether or not I was telling the truth, he said,

"O.K! But don't try nothin.'"

After knocking on the door a few times I could hear Beverly's footsteps nearing. I prayed even harder she would look through the peephole in the door and see what was going on before opening it, and that death was about to enter with me if she let me in.

The sound of her footsteps stopped. The peephole in the door swiveled and the first latch clicked. *Shit!* It became obvious to me she hadn't seen what was jumping off. The heavy bar of the police lock slid into the door-opening position and stopped; the door began opening. I then knew for sure; she didn't see things coming.

With a sudden force, both of the men pushed me through the door, pinning her behind it. The fifty or so years that should have been remaining in my life suddenly turned to seconds. My only chance was the gun in her hand. As I strained to reach around the door she still couldn't actually see what was going on.

Reaching out for her hand where the pistol should have been, the gunman swung around in back of me. It became obvious I was doing what I had been warned not to do. In the haste, there were three hands on the gun I was reaching for, mine, hers, and the one that held the knife in my back.

POW!

The sound echoed through the apartment. Suddenly it felt like someone forced a red-hot poker through my back and into my stomach. I was no longer a threat as I fell to the floor. Bev didn't stand a chance at that point, losing a portion of the tip of her finger as it tangled in the trigger when the gun was yanked from her hand.

With the noise from the gunfire, it would be too risky for them to stay any longer. They left; their only take being the five-shot pistol they lucked out on. Lying there on the floor I saw my life pass before me. The only vision was my mother, dealing with the reality her young and only son had been killed in a dope house – dying with my shoes on like my father did.

Lying on the floor, burning inside, the main thought that crossed my mind was Nan. I knew she loved me and this was no way to pay her back for all the things she'd done for me in my life. I thought about not seeing my sister, Deb, again and how she would feel knowing her only brother was dead. The only thing bringing comfort was that I'd saved the lives of the innocent women and children I was protecting.

It seemed like it took forever for the emergency wagon to show up. I figured when Will was able to walk away from the scene he went and knocked on someone's door to get help or call the police. His call should have given the police and paramedics a head start in getting there to probably what he figured may have been my last moments.

Finally the paramedics arrived after what seemed like an hour though it was about twenty minutes. The police showed up within a couple of minutes. Groaning in pain, the medics removed the coat that only showed a spot of blood and began looking for the wound and the damage it caused. They noticed there was no blood oozing through the bullet hole in my back after finding it, which meant I was bleeding internally. They began to rush getting me on the stretcher and down the stairs to the ambulance. The pain never eased. It seemed the heat caused by the bullet remained constant.

They put me in the ambulance and took me to the Emergency Room at Henry Ford Hospital, which was less than five miles away. It seemed it took forever to get there irrespective of the fact they didn't stop or slow for anything. They knew my life was on the line and did all they could to save it. When we reached the hospital they rushed me out of the wagon and inside. It appeared they had the whole Emergency Room staff was waiting for me. I was rushed into room number one, the room they used for the most traumatic situations and emergencies. When they pushed me in the only thing visible were the bright overhead lights hanging from the ceiling. They didn't ask any questions, just began cutting off all my clothes with scissors.

The pain only seemed to get worse and more aggravating as I lay there on the table. Before they could do anything they had to get x-rays of the injury to see just what damage had occurred and how they would attempt to keep me living.

"Put me to sleep!" I said.

"We can't. If we do you might slip into a coma and we can't take that chance," one of the doctors responded.

I thought I would never be able to make it through all the pain and internal bleeding. I knew I'd be dead by the time they got me to the operating room.

When the doctors got the result of the x-rays they saw the injuries were too difficult for any of the resident doctors to handle, saying the bullet had twisted and bound my intestines up in knots and that there were injuries to my kidneys and liver. They said they would have to call in one of the few doctors they had on staff who could handle such a surgery. He was nowhere around and we would have to wait for him to come from home. The pain only increased.

"Please put me to sleep. I can't stand the pain," I begged.

I had no other choice but to lay there and deal with it. No matter how much I begged, they wouldn't even consider putting me under while they waited for the doctor to show. I just lay there, feeling the warmth of the blood filling inside.

By the time the surgeon showed up they had me prepped and ready to go straight into the O.R. Lying on my back, only seeing the ceilings and lights above, they rolled me on the gurney upstairs and taken into the operating room. Finally, I knew comfort was coming in the way of anesthesia.

Inside the operating room they hooked up machines and monitors to my lifeless body. I could see nothing but a bright light, not caused by incandescence, but a light that was more like a bright sun. Then everything faded to black.

CHAPTER 6: ANOTHER CHANCE

A glimpse of light peering from the hallway in a darkened room imaged a figure in the distance, wearing a glowing white bonnet. As my eyes widened I could see it was a nurse sitting at a desk, directly across a hall. There was no light coming in the windows, indicating it was at least late evening after the early winter sunset. The only lights in the room were cast from all the different machines and monitors. I was still too sedated to feel any pain. There were other beds in the same dark ward with other lifeless figures resembling corpses in a morgue. Nobody moved. It was obvious though that if I was alive, all of them were suffering near death traumas and were clinging on to life like me. I realized I'd be around a little longer.

I couldn't do much more than look at the ceiling over my bed. Struggling to move my head to make out my surroundings, a shadow stood up next to me. Before making out the identity of the figure I heard Bev's voice. When she came closer to the bed I made an attempt to reach out with a grasp of desperation. She smiled stingily when she stood over me. She looked like she had been there in that chair all day. No words came from my lips when calling for them. I was happy to see her but there were tubes running through my nose and down my throat, containing my speech. It was now New Year's Eve night, three days since seeing her last.

I stayed awake for about fifteen or so minutes then went back to sleep.

The next time my eyes opened there were white silhouettes hovering over me. I was in a room full of what looked like angels. What appeared to be seraphs though were doctors dressed in their white coats, standing, looking at me like a scientific undertaking that had been miraculously executed.

I was.

Fortunately it wasn't destined for me to die at that time. Once again I was greatly blessed, this time getting a renewal of life. My surgeon explained it was my abnormally strong heart that kept me alive; actually, my heart *did* stop and had to be resuscitated. Almost gone, I came out of it but not without going through about eight pints of blood, mostly because of internal bleeding.

The doctors began their examination of me. The first thing in the inspection was my feet, checking to see if I had feeling in them, which would reveal whether or not paralysis was in my legs. Dr. Block, the doctor who did the surgery, told me the bullet that entered my back nicked my spine, and that if it had been a quarter of an inch closer I would have undoubtedly been paralyzed from the waist down.

I was a newer version of young Frankenstein, mummified with bandages and wraps, covering my whole upper torso. While removing the bandages he explained the damages. I'd lost half of one kidney, a piece of my liver, and about five feet of my large intestine because the impact from the bullet twisted them into knots.

As he removed some of the bandages I could see what looked like my intestines protruding through my stomach. They were. It was the result of a procedure called a colostomy, a bypass of the bowel that allowed the damaged part of the organs to heal. It complemented the raggedness of my once smooth virgin looking stomach, confirming they didn't waste any time cutting me open and closing me back. Wire stitches retained the hide of my belly together, while a parallel row of what looked like firecrackers with thick jade-color ropes that looked like fuses running through them held my internal organs intact. There were also drainage tubes running out of both of my sides.

Dr. Block, who, at that time was notably one of the best surgeons in Detroit's *Henry Ford Hospital*, had saved my life. He explained the bag would have to be worn for a while in order to pass my stool. The feeling was better off dead. I was too young to go through life like that, and too immature to conceive the idea. Sparing me, he added in his belief it should only be five months, temporary. Thank God. He also told me of the injuries caused to my internal organs including my liver, and that the kidney they operated on was the one healthiest. He said I might live only twelve to twenty years from the injuries.

The first few days of my new life were faint. I felt like all of my insides had been ripped out of me, stuffed back in, and sewn into place. Tubes ran in and out of every part of my body one could be put. The only place I didn't have a tube was in my butt. And there was no need for that because my colon had been disconnected. Stomach pumps, electrodes and tubes led from my lifeless body to a number of monitors and machines. One of them worked like an air conditioning unit that cooled thermal pads, which lay under me, keeping my body temperature normal. Two IV poles held plasma, saline and meds that dripped through tubes and into my arm.

The hardest part of recovery was getting out of the bed and walking after only a few days since surgery. From the way I felt walking was beyond conception. Though realizing I'd have to get out the bed eventually, my body couldn't answer the call. With all the tubes attached I figured they'd let me slide for a few days, but one of the nurses let me know I'd have to walk. They disconnected everything that could be and made me get up and on my feet. At first there were two nurses walking me because my legs were too weak to hold me up.

Every time I moved it hurt. I felt like puking at times with the smell of the hospital and the tube down my throat working in conjunction with making me more sick. The pole that held the intravenous bags of life sustaining fluids became a crutch for me to make it down the long hall, managing to take a few more steps each time I walked. After fighting to regain my strength I began watching television, annoyed by characters in Westerns getting shot with .44's, riding fifty miles to the town doctor, and back on their horses the next day. I felt like throwing something at the tube but didn't have strength to pick anything up. The acting on the screen was nothing like the real thing; neither was that .22, wondering if this was punishment for shooting myself.

About ten days after my first strides I was able to walk the whole distance of the entire corridor. Every day my walks became faster and faster. Once learning the importance of walking and how it would affect my recovery, nobody had to tell me to get up and make the stroll. Actually it was the only thing for me to do. It got to the point I was almost jogging in the halls with the I.V. pole at my side. Staying in the sickbay became like being in a jail; walking was the only escape.

Beginning to feel much better and no longer having to use an I.V. pole when walking, I walked the whole hospital until covering almost every inch of it. I was feeling fine and ready to go home. I'd even gotten used to using the bathroom in a bag. My stay in the hospital was a couple days short of a month. Moving around freely I wanted to go home and finish recuperating and get back to making money and saving my job. I had been off a month.

* * *

Norman ran the business for a while until getting someone else, a guy named Rob who was already a sometime client and brother to a few customers who had become friends. Norman had excelled in the business to the degree that he was beyond running a small change business. He was primarily dealing with customers who bought large amounts at the place he'd moved into around the corner.

Upon returning home from the hospital I was still in no shape to return to work. Norman got another apartment on W. Chicago, only a few blocks away from the apartment. It took me a few months to walk straight and fully upright instead of the bent over hunchback position. I started visiting Norman and Bert at a new home they bought on the Westside of the city. Rob ran the business and could see myself losing out. I asked Norman if my spot would still be available when I was ready to come back to work. He couldn't give me a straight answer until Bert found out. When she did she hit the ceiling. He said he didn't want to change things now that he had someone already handling things. Besides, it would still be quite a while before I would be able to handle things.

Big Daddy gave Beverly and me a place to stay while I was recuperating from having my colon put back in order. He had a two-family flat conveniently located a quarter mile from the hub. I stayed at Nan's for a while until I felt like moving into the upstairs flat and walking the stairs.

* * *

It took a while for me to get my strength back over the months to come. I'd lost at least twenty of my one hundred and forty pounds. I almost looked like Norman's twin; he was hardly bigger than Nan except for about two inches taller. While regaining my vigor and weight, television became a major pastime. When lying up in the hospital the first time, I picked up the habit of watching soap operas. I got addicted to them like most of us had become addicted to the influences of song and media.

Music, fashion, television, and senseless trends were dominating the seventies. For many it was all about the "*Brady Bunch*," pet rocks, discotheques, CB radios, mood rings, and jumpsuits, but the prime influences (mostly for the worst) in the Black community were movies like "*Superfly*" and "*The Mack.*" These movies were major ingredients of self-destruction, leaving us believing that hustling in the streets was the best way to get rich and buy a Cadillac. As if that were the only thing we needed in life and a way out of the ghetto. To date, many of us still live the same dream. Of the many people who lost their lives or put them on the line for the quick dollar most no longer have a penny of the money they made. They died with their dreams, only passing the ideology down through generations.

Watching the tube was a major pastime mania, along with music and discos. Whether it was *Welcome Back, Kotter, Kojak,* or *Sanford and Son,* we all found something worth watching the fictitious worlds of characters generated by Hollywood's best. Many of us began devoting eight and ten hours a day and more, sitting in front of the idiot box, not aware of the psychological effects we would suffer from living in a fantasy world of women, drugs, fast money, and gangsters.

Some of us picked up new personalities from the characters we adored on the screen. Many found it difficult to separate reality from fiction, taking part in the imaginary. Movies with gun toting personalities portrayed by tough guys like Charles Bronson and Clint Eastwood gave one ultimate satisfaction in the thrill of seeing someone bust a cap in somebody's face.

Along with gunfire and deaths of those on the screen came the disregard for life. Many became eager to practice the methods of killing and victimizing they saw two nights prior while watching the *Sunday Night Movie.* What we didn't realize is that we inadvertently retained traits of some actor we saw on TV or at the movies. These people emulating characters of the screen began strolling city streets, portrayed by the latest additions to the hoodlum world, the ghetto gangster and the coward using a gun to take advantage of someone who didn't have one. Like fast hope with dope, this manipulation has also been passed down.

One of the most moving scenes of disregard for Black life came from the movie *The Godfather,* in which Don Corleone and other mafia heads discussed where to distribute illegal and highly addictive narcotics. The Don was opposed to the distribution and involvement with drugs. One of the family heads, which was in favor of the distribution plan suggested that distribution should be isolated to the Black neighborhoods because "they are animals." I never understood the logic behind such a statement being used. It may have been an application of reverse psychology to intimidate us out of using drugs by placing a stigma that we would be pigeonholed with savagery if we did. Whatever the reason, we found more value in the foreboding scene of the horse owner who woke up with the decapitated head of his prize mare in his bed.

* * *

After really getting back on my feet I worked part time at the apartment with Rob for a while until Bert decided to have me work for them alone, delivering packages and running errands. Sometimes I flew to New York and California to make transactions. Norman was buying a new Fleetwood every year, and even a Rolls Royce. Every now and then I'd chauffer him around in the Rolls. Bert didn't like the idea of being too flamboyant but it was Norman's way. It didn't matter to me because I was getting paid and had a heroin habit to support.

Things continued to go good in the business for a couple of years, until Bert found out Norman was having an affair with a girl I went to school with who I'd introduced to him back in the apartment on Lawton three years prior. Learning he had been cheating on her with a young lady I went to school with only made it worse. She went to the largest of the two safety deposit boxes, emptied it and left town, leaving him with enough to start over without her connections. With her gone and Norman being suckered in by a young lady who had her eye on the prize from day one, it was time for me to move on; time to start my own business. The problem was not having any connects to buy my drugs from. Now that Bert was gone Norman had to rely on local contacts that caused him to spiral downward, supporting his and his new lady's habit.

The spot on Gladstone became my new home with Bev and her two children. I had become the father figure to both her son and daughter. The need to make money to take care of a family left me forced to find the connections and clientele needed to start my own business. Though it was still selling drugs, it was my job and the lazy way to make money. I had skills to find a job in the trade I learned, but kept the hardheaded attitude to keep hustling. Nan offered to buy me a truck and help me start a business because she said working for someone else is something she couldn't see me doing. While the offer was good, drugs were my game, figuring I could get paid like many were still doing.

One day while visiting my mother and a few old friends on the street I grew up on I saw one of Charles' ladies driving a new Lincoln. Charles had moved off Glynn before the time I got shot. When I saw Wanda, his money honey, driving the car I figured it was his, but was surprised to see him with a ride like that. Asking where he was and telling her that I wanted to see him, She gave me his number.

Seeing Charles I was truly surprised to discover that he'd bought the car with drug money he'd earned during the time I'd spent in the last two years working with Bert and Norm. I knew pimping was his hustle, but at the time he taught us to play Blackjack I never would have suspected he would be selling heroin; he seemed a little too old for that venue. He told me how long he'd been on the square and that he had a connection with some Mexicans that were supplying him with a product he could cut ten times and still have a quality product.

Over the months to come not only did I buy from Charles, but found it necessary to meet several connects. When one dried up I found another. Once Charles and me made a run to Chicago to make a buy after I built up enough money to buy a few ounces. Money was coming in; I remodeled the flat we lived in and gave it a total transformation, suspending the ceilings, adding cork and mirrors to the walls, installing a bar counter and bar stools, new lighting, carpet, wallpaper and a hell of a lock on the door to keep the police from kicking it in.

My friends and money grew simultaneously. Customers that I hadn't seen in a while appeared. Many of the people who were part of the family we had established before Norman got lost on a skirt tail became my regulars. When Bert came back to town to take care of some unfinished business she had before leaving, she brought out old heads that used to get dope from her on consignment. We even had a party where I was the one this time to hand out free dope like Norman did years prior.

At the party one of the guys Norman and Bert knew from New York, and brought along, Charlie Hawkins, introduced me to a guy known as Train, also from upstate New York, like Bert, but from Niagara Falls. He was an older guy at least in his fifties, with his seasoning gray hair cut close. He had astigmatism; one of his eyes went one way and the other went another. When he looked at you it was hard to know if he was looking at you or somewhere else. It was obvious he didn't use any drugs and was in the game strictly for the money. Charlie was hoping I would be a contact for him to buy his quinine and Dormin, which was used to cut his dope for the shooters he sold to back in New York. Almost everyone from Niagara Falls was shooting heroin because of the cost allowing them to get all of their money's worth. Train had already got his dope but he needed the other stuff before making his trip back home.

When the drug store opened the next day after the party I was there, buying what my new contact wanted. The store was known for selling all the hard to find adulterates. I got what he asked for and took it back to him. He was happier than a kid with a new toy because he had no other way to get the stuff because his suppliers couldn't be found. He wanted to know if I could supply him with some powder as well. I explained my thing wasn't quantities but could probably accommodate him if he didn't need more than an ounce.

Eventually he came and bought drugs from me and took them back to New York and made ten times the money I was making on the same goods. When he came into town I went and bought his quinine and Dormin, a sleep aid that was added to street mix to give it an added effect. When he came he came through Canada. He knew all the people who worked Customs and had a way to get back home via a bridge that was the safest. He turned out to be one of my best customers, spending the most money when he came to town. I had everything going in my favor until my habit and need for drugs caught up with me.

CHAPTER 7: THE SECOND FELONY

I ran into my old friend Leonard one day. I hadn't seen him since Theodore died. He was a good friend of Pee Wee's, Theodore's brother and had been a periodic customer before I got shot. He was driving a very sharp new Oldsmobile ninety-eight. It was triple red and had a half-top with a moon roof and leather seats. I invited him to come by the place where I lived and he did. He wasn't a regular user like me, but for him it was more like an occasional drink. He seemed to be doing quite well. He was still with the same young lady he had been with all his life. They had gotten married and had a child together.

After we had a number of encounters he revealed to me that he wanted to get rid of his car. I couldn't figure out why he wanted to get rid of it because it was still like new. The thought entertained me, as my love affair with cars had never ceased from when I learned so much about them as a kid visiting the General Motors building every week during my two years of confirmation classes. I'd stop on my way home and visit the massive showrooms that displayed all the makes and models they sold.

"Get rid of it how?" I asked him.

"However I can! I'd like to do an insurance job with it."

I knew that getting rid of an automobile to have the insurance company pay for it usually meant stripping it to the point where the car was classified "totaled" so that the owner or lien holder would be paid in full. The car was so beautiful I couldn't see it being stripped. I told him I would take it though, after learning he had a friend working in the DMV and could get me some plates and a registration for it.

No sooner than getting the paperwork for me to drive the car safely I was rolling in the sharpest ride ever. While we left the numbers unchanged on the VIN, I figured the police would never investigate once handing them a registration with my name on it and the plates also registered to the vehicle. Once having the paperwork, it felt like I had bought and paid for it. It was the car that could be placed alongside all the others that were able to buy flashy rides with their dope money. Leonard wasn't in the dope game, but had the car, at least until I got it.

* * *

Business went on as usual. Train continued coming my way and helped increase my income along with the other customers who were becoming regulars to the point I could depend on them to support me and keep my business going. After Train made a number of trips he stopped buying from me; a connection he had in Niagara Falls was able to supply him with a nice quantity that would last him for a while, but he still needed the quinine and Dormin. He told me that if I was having trouble making my buys here in Detroit I could come there and get something from him, but told me if I ever came that way to take a particular bridge because there weren't many Canadian customs officers at that exit entering back into the U.S. I didn't see going though, I was still getting what I needed without taking the chances he did; nobody would have ever suspected him by looking at him.

Within a month of Train's last trip my contacts dried up and the offer he made me began to have appeal. I called him and let him know I'd be coming to pay him a visit. I got maps from my insurance company that were free and gave me mapped out directions how to get there. He told me upon arrival to call his daughter and to go to her house and he would then contact me. From there, the idea was to make my transactions quickly and be on my way to make the three hundred and fifty mile run back home. The only difference would be on the way back I would travel through the U.S., avoiding Canadian borders.

The quickest transportation available was the ninety-eight, thinking the bus run would add on another day to my trip, riding on an uncomfortable bench seat. The run seemed like a must since not finding what I needed to keep my business going. I decided to drive it, figuring my paperwork to the car would be good in case Customs questioned me. Not knowing how long or when I'd be able to get some dope upon getting there, taking my own didn't require much deliberation. I figured hiding some of the small amount of narcotics somewhere in the car for my personal use was something achievable.

Thinking of a lot of places to hide something in the car, the idea to hide it in the door in a cigarette pack was where I ended. The amount was only for personal use, and a portion of what was left at home. I removed the hand-cove out that sat behind the door handle from the inside and found a resting place that was perfect between steel grids. I placed the package carefully and screwed the chrome cup back into its place.

Around midnight, I kissed Beverly goodbye and my journey began. I filled the car with gas and made the ten-minute ride to the border. When entering Canada it only took a few minutes to hit the 401, a major highway that runs through much of the province that leads to Toronto and beyond. The night travel around all the waterways in Canada along with the right conditions led to a highway full of fog with almost zero visibility.

As dawn broke the end of my journey through Canada was near. The weather was nice and the sun was beginning to pierce the clouds. It was only thirty or so miles to the border when I started seeing signs that gave me directions to the way leading back into the U.S. I didn't know exactly which way to get to the crossing that Train had told me about. It was the Bluewater Bridge and I couldn't tell if the signs for that viaduct were the ones tofollow. In desperation of getting back into the U.S. my memory became cloudy, and I couldn't remember if it was that bridge for sure. It sounded right. There was no way for me to call – no cell phones.

When the exit for the bridge approached I took it, heading toward the U.S. border. As the Customs booths came in sight, the closer I got I could read the letters adhered to the huge canopy on the plaza overhead; it read RAINBOW BRIDGE. My foot gently began engaging the brake.

"Shit! I got the wrong damn bridge!"

It was too late to turn back around. If I did I know I'd have all the Canadian Mounties in the region chasing me for sure.

I proceeded to the Customs booth.

"Good morning, sir," the female officer greeted.

"Good morning!" I replied.

"You're a citizen of what country, sir?"

"U.S."

"How long have you been in Canada?" she asked.

"Just traveling through," I replied.

She began looking in the back seat as the next words came from her mouth.

"Are you bringing anything out of Canada to declare, sir?"

'No.'

"Would you open the trunk for me?"

"Sure," I said.

I reached into the glove box to push the trunk release button. The lid popped and she opened it and looked inside for only a brief moment.

"Pull over to the side, sir." She pointed in the direction where officers usually wind up questioning you more and then eventually they search.

Fuck, why did she pull me over so quick when she looked in the trunk? I wondered for a second before answering the question myself. *There's nothing in it!*

DAMN! That's why, fool! You don't have any goddamn luggage! Who in the hell goes on a trip without some type of luggage or clothes bags?

It was too late. All I could do was hope they didn't get as far as to tear the car apart if they searched it. By the time I made it over to the area I was directed, my heart rate had doubled. Out of all the things I'd learned to do well in my life, lying wasn't one of them.

The agents took me into a room and began questioning me if I was bringing anything in or out of the country. Not taking my word for it they began to search me. They searched well, from my long permed hair to the seams on my clothes and found nothing, not even a weed seed. But something they knew; that I was dirty in some way, having well over a thousand dollars cash in my pocket. I guessed they saw it on my face or could hear the thumps of my heart. They asked me for the registration to the car. Giving it to them they matched them to the VIN numbers on the dashboard, and of course, they matched.

Though I had been searched and the numbers on the vehicle matched, they still weren't satisfied. They took both the vehicle and me into a garage.

Shit! I know they have to find that damn dope if they start tearing this car apart!

Once they began the search I knew they were going to find that damn cigarette pack. While it wasn't much real heroin with all the cut, it was enough to get my ass some very serious time. I didn't have enough sense to avoid the situation, but had enough sense to know doing time in a foreign jail was imminent.

The officers opened everything on the car that could be, doors, hood, trunk lid, and even the moon roof. They searched for twenty minutes before they eventually got the idea to call in and check on the car to see if it could have been stolen. After their call to the U.S., they asked me if I had just bought the car or something because it was a stolen vehicle. I told them that I had bought it a couple of months prior. At that point I knew I was busted.

They asked me whom I bought the car from and was suddenly caught off guard, figuring if mentioning Leonard, it would implicate him so they got one of those dumb fictitious names like Ed Brown or something. They asked me if I knew a Leonard Thompson. *Damn!*

"No" I told them, knowing if I said yes, they would still be suspicious because it was still on the hot-sheet.

That was when they began a second search of the car. The attitude they had was that they weren't going to give up until they could figure out why I was making my trip and that it was either dope related or an auto theft ring.

By then my brown face had probably turned beige. They resumed their search; this time with tools and flashlights, taking everything loose that would be loosened. Under the hood they did everything but check the oil, and the same for the trunk except breaking down the tire. Though they still found nothing, they still explored. When the agent opened the passenger door and let the window down I turned from light brown to blue. Once he made it to the driver's door he was about to find that cigarette pack without a doubt. He took his flashlight and angled it down through the crack where the window retracts. It seemed like he looked for five minutes and found nothing. As expected, he proceeded around the car to the other door and began the same type of search. Again, he looked for what seemed like several minutes. I could hear his unspoken words.

"I found something!"

No more colors; I nearly shit and peed on myself at the same time as by body turned to Jell-O. The agent took his flashlight and aimed it at the hole and shined the beam of light into the area where the cigarette pack was and looked in. My insides started to cry. It was a miracle he didn't see that big box when he looked down in the door between the panels, but he didn't and they finished the search, leaving me with a slight sigh of relief until he went to the inside of the door and began removing the chrome recess behind the door handle. After a moment of looking he took the chrome cup and screwed it back into place. I almost passed out from relief.

Learning auto body repair in school may have helped, but whatever it was it saved me for sure. I had to deal with somebody about the car, but not the dope. They called the police in Niagara Falls, who came for me because the incident was U.S. related. The police and the tow truck arrived at about the same. Sitting in the back of the car I watched as the front of my full size coupe was raised with the hook. Only having the car a few months; watching the grill go in the air gave me the feeling of losing something more than I ever had, and something never earned. One thing was for sure; when I got back home I wouldn't have a car and would have to explain to everyone what happened to my new ride.

By the time the police officers both entered the vehicle, with me in the back, the only thing on my mind was how those officers didn't find that dope. If they had found it they would have charged me with smuggling heroin, a charge that would have made me an old man in the clink and I wouldn't be headed back to the States. We left the bridge with the tow truck following, my car on the hook. I couldn't help but to smile though, which turned to an internal chuckle. The officer who was driving, looking through his rear view mirror replied,

"Are you ok back there? You seem to be about the happiest man we ever took to jail!"

* * *

When getting to jail in the Falls on the U.S. side, the questioning began. They wanted to know where I was going and who seeing.

"My cousin here in the city." I lied.

They made their reports as we talked. After they didn't buy my story they brought in detectives who questioned me even more. Eventually they gave me a cell and the chance to make a few phone calls. My first one was made to Beverly to let her know of my fuck up and that it may be a while before making it back home. The next call was to Train's daughter Debbie, to get a message to him of what had happened and to be on standby to bail me out if it came to that, not knowing if I would be spending days in lockup or months. There was no answer.

They took me to my temporary holding place. After a couple of hours passed they gave me the opportunity to let me try and make my call again. There was still no answer. Hesitating, the next call was to Train. He wasn't at home but his wife was. I asked her what the best time to reach him was. She told me when he gets off work at about four, only a couple hours away. My thoughts became overwhelming of the mistakes made through the influences and encumbrances of drugs. Withdrawals fueled the anguish of being locked in a cell without a snort of my usual medicine, something that was in my hand whenever I had wanted for years without end. The recollections of the loss of my car and the need for dope left my thoughts in a ping-pong match. Knowing Train would find out my trip to see him to buy drugs was made with a stolen car, the feelings from withdrawals coincided with shame even though he hadn't found out yet.

My craving left me wishing I had the stuff hidden in the car door as much as having the car. The hard bench that rested my meatless hips added injury to the insult. A puppy in a pen replaced the big dog in the hood. The thing to do now was to begin conditioning my mind to deal with being locked up for perhaps years, and most, being away from Beverly and not seeing my mother, who was then entering her seventies. Once again, I looked at the possibilities of her being traumatized by her 'wanna' be dope dealing son. Telling her I was a fixture in an out of state prison was something that would shave years off her life worrying about me.

Back in my cell about forty-five minutes later, the detectives decided to question me again about my reason for being there in the Falls with a stolen car. This time they had some photos of mug shots upside down on the table where we sat. They turned over one of them and asked me if I knew the gentleman on the picture.

"I don't recognize this person."

They turned over another; it was Train. *Damn! These motherfuckers done traced my phone call and now they know whom I was coming to see. Shit! You dumb motherfucker you done fucked up again! Damn!*

"Do you know him?" one of the detectives asked, knowing that I had some type of association with him because they had apparently traced the call.

"He's my uncle!" I said answering with the only lie that came to mind and something that corresponded to the first lie of visiting my cousin.

My retort must have been questionable according to the look on their faces when they looked at each other and grimaced. The questioning continued, suggesting me being a hit man in town to do a hit on Train. They said my hard looks helped me fit the description of an assassin. Maybe it was the stony look heroin addicts get. Things had now gone in a whole different direction, knowing they were playing head games trying to force out my real reason for being there. They knew who Train was and knew things about him because they had his mug with a number and a name I never knew him by. They persisted with their interrogation until it got them nowhere. They locked me back up in the cell.

Dinnertime turned out to be a king's meal in a jailhouse; a burger with a lukewarm order of fries and a container of milk. I knew the meals would soon change from fast food and Pringles to shit on shingles. I guessed the meal was a way of opening me up to talk a little more, but they could have fed me filet mignon; they weren't about to squeeze me. After eating the luscious meal I took my place on the bunk, runny nose, tearing eyes and all the symptoms of a junkie needing a fix.

Turnkey came and opened my cell about eight in the evening and took me to the booking room, telling me on the way I'd been released on a writ. Once the officer who manned the desk handed my property back as it was left, belt, shoestrings, money and all, I knew it wasn't another trick for getting me to talk. Happy to be out under any condition for a moment was a dream, but took a lawyer to get a writ of habeas corpus, which also took money and sometimes pull. While relieved, I knew that Train was the only one who could have pulled those strings. It became more than a notion that he was a lot more than a tastelessly dressed old man pushing a few bags of dope, giving me a feeling of being the grim reaper's next victim.

Sitting on the bench, lacing my shoes and putting my things back where they belonged, the thoughts of who was waiting on me on the other side of the jailhouse walls remained a mystery. I figured it wouldn't be Train. The amazement by the quickness I was released and being the time of day it was, which was after business hours, ruled my consciousness. Nevertheless, I laced, strapped, and headed towards the door to freedom.

When walking through the door a full-figured young lady who looked like she had been dipped in sweet dark chocolate was the only person in the lobby. When getting within a few feet of her she questioned with a jovial smile.

"You must be Sonny?"

"Yes."

Countering cheerfully as if she already had known me for years.

"I'm Deb! Come and go with me. I'm going to take you to my house. You have a ten 'o clock appointment with the lawyer in the morning. You'll stay at my house tonight."

Lawyer? How the hell did I get a lawyer when I didn't have money for one?

Train!

Walking quietly with her to the parking lot I didn't have much to say with egg all over my face. She seemed almost twice my size and weight and though I was at her side she didn't seem to need me as her escort. We got in her car and drove off.

The ride didn't twist many words from Train's daughter. The most she did was smile with her pudgy cheeks with smiles that forced dimples into her smooth skinned face. I didn't know what to say or where to begin a conversation. The only thing I could think about was what was on her father's mind.

"I know your father is pissed off at me?" Probing.

She tilted her head to the lower left and then said, "Yeah, I guess you could say that!"

I felt that sometime in the near future I would be scolded like a kid who breaks a window after he's been told not to play ball. The only escape was temporary refuge at Deb's house for the night.

We rode for over a half hour before reaching her house. Along the way she told me that she had just gotten cable TV installed, something we didn't have yet back in Detroit. She said it didn't work all the time though because they hadn't yet worked all the bugs out. While television was a good idea, my concentration was more on getting some dope to feel normal. It was obvious she was like her dad and didn't use anything other than the food they both seemed to love shown by the few extra pounds in reserve.

The next morning Debbie took me to see the lawyer who obviously pulled a few strings to get me out before a court appearance. Having less than a grand in my pocket, hiring this guy would be a lot more than what I had or could raise. When walking into his office I noticed a very clean-cut Caucasian gentleman wearing a dark suit, very expensive suit. His tie was blue silk and his haircut looked like he paid his barber every bit of a hundred bucks for it. The gloss on his shoes didn't reflect even the dust picked up off the Persian carpeted floor.

"My name is Rocco Corruno! I've been hired by Ed Brammel to represent you."

I know this motherfucker 'gon break my ass. Sharp as this dude is he needs the money in my pocket to buy his lunch!

After talking rhetoric a while I still couldn't focus on anything other than the dollar signs floating in sight. The question floating most was,

"How much are your fees?" I asked him almost as scared to hear his recrimination. He responded quickly as a hungry person saying yes to free food.

"Two hundred and fifty dollars an hour. And don't worry about today; it's taken care of already by Mr. Brammel," he said.

The self-painting picture detailed the identity of the subject, Train, someone who wasn't just a nickel dime hustler but someone who had clout, and a lot of it. I had brought heat on someone who had nothing to do with my stupidity. If he hadn't been someone being investigated by the police, now it was a good possibility of them investigating further. When the lawyer and me finished our conversation I left the office, not knowing when I'd have to appear in court. Mr. Corruno told me that I should have an arraignment the next day and that I'd have to stay in town and appear before the judge to get a bond.

I spent the next several hours wishing to undo everything done and thinking how and what to say to Train when seeing him later that day after he got off work. If he had been a wanted man the police would now be on his trail, and if I had never made the trip, his mug shot would never have been pulled. The next few hours were spent watching television, feeling like a kid about to be scolded by his father. The difference was that Train was a total stranger. Still, it wasn't in me to run and leave him on the spot so I waited for him to arrive.

It was before four-thirty when the key slid into the lock cylinder, the door opening afterwards. Train walked into the room and his daughter walked out. I could see the anger on his face and the fire in his eyes. He didn't hesitate before the first words fired from his lips.

"Alright, the first thing you did wrong was come over here to see me in a stolen goddamn car! The next thing was to call me from the police station! They got them phones tapped and they know you called my house! And why didn't you use the bridge I told you to?"

I suddenly had the ambition to find any small bug in the room and crawl up its ass. He looked at me straining to keep both eyes in my direction. I didn't know which one to look in but I wanted to make sure he knew he had my attention so I paralleled between the two.

"Let me tell you something, man! These police have been trying to get me for years. They know who I am and I know most of them. They also probably know why you came here to see me!"

"I apologize. You're right. I fucked up bad and I know it. I didn't mean to get you involved in my stupidity," I remarked.

My comments did not change his facial gestures at all. He looked like if I had been his son he probably would have knocked the shit out of me.

"Come on," he told me.

"Deb! I'll be back later," he shouts.

We left the house and headed for his car.

"I've got to go to Buffalo and take care of some business," he said.

We walked outside to arrive at his old Chevy Malibu that looked like a car that belonged to someone who could barely afford one. It was the same car he drove all the way to Detroit routinely. If he was a big dope man you couldn't tell by the clothes he wore and his ride. The four-door sedan was at least fifteen years old and had a lean of its own that complemented the rear passenger side. The motor, though, ran like a sewing machine. It was so quiet you couldn't even hear it run. It reminded me of the cars bootleggers used to run moonshine, where the motor was more important than looks and always had a fresh overhaul. The coveralls he wore gave him a slight sense of tawdriness, not linking to any edition of a fashion trend. His short-cut partially gray hair gave kinship to his factory work clothes, making him look like the upstanding Joe Neighbor on any street in a decent neighborhood.

He seemed to cool off quickly as he began telling me things about himself I never suspected. The police had not only wanted him for being a drug dealer, but he had been a key figure in an unsolved robbery twenty years prior. He and two other guys pulled off the rip without getting caught, but they knew he had something to do with it because he had just gotten out of jail for the same thing. The police knew he was involved because he was the only one known suspect that had the skills to crack the safe. He wasn't a drug dealer by trade but an expert B&E man.

We reached Buffalo about an hour after we left Niagara Falls. Train had an aunt who lived in a house he owned. I didn't know the reason for making the long trip for something other than retrieving some powder he stashed there, but it looked like he just went there to check on her. After being there only a few minutes we left, headed back to the Falls where he lived, worked and played.

When we got back he took me to his home. I went inside with him and greeted his wife and dog. She was the type of woman who made him look even more innocent than the cheap coveralls he wore. She looked just like the average auntie; the press and curled hair, the comfort shoes and eyeglasses. I sat on the couch for a minute while he went out in the backyard for a moment, quickly returning. We went into the basement of the where he brought out the package he apparently dug up when he went outside. He didn't seem to care much if the stuff would get damp from moisture and the rain, but he must have had faith in the way it was packaged.

He brought out his tools, a plate, the quinine and Dormin he often traveled to Detroit to get, and the dope he already had. While my eyes still watered and my nose continued to sniffle, suffering from the withdrawals of a three-day cold turkey, I was tempted to ask him for some of the raw dog he had on the table. He didn't use anything and I would also have added the name junkie to the list of my other accumulative errs if I asked for some dope to feel normal again. As bad as I wanted to ask, I didn't.

After Train finished mixing his batch for the night we left the house and jumped into his hooptie. He took me for a ride on a route he drove to handle his customers, showing me how they were never able to catch him dirty because he kept the drug packages inside of a balled up empty cigarette pack. He told me that if the police ever attempted to pull him over he would simply toss the package out the window, claiming that even if they did see him throw it out they would have to prove it was his and that whatever happened the stuff wouldn't be found on him.

I sat in the passenger seat as we began driving his course, which gave me the chance to view some unseen streets and how the Train stayed on the tracks. After driving only a few minutes to the first spot, the first customer came up to the ride after he stopped. A young lady walked up to the car and got a sixty-dollar package. We rode a few blocks before he made another stop. After about fifteen minutes it was like I was actually riding on a train, making routine stops, picking up money instead of passengers. Before I could ask how he got in the dope game, he opened up.

He told me he took up selling drugs after his two partners began spending their share of the loot from the robbery on drugs. Once he saw how much money they were wasting getting high, he bought some dope, sold it to them and got all of the money. Once they were broke he kept on selling. The years that passed since the incident didn't make a difference, they still wanted him, and even more now because he was the town's main drug supplier but never could catch him. Of all their many attempted searches and seizures they never got a case on him because they never found any dope.

The more we drove the more people came up to the car when he stopped. In some cases the wheels never stopped rolling because the transactions were as if they were timed. If you missed the train you had to wait until the next pass. In less than an hour he picked up at least a thousand dollars from the fiends in the streets. It was obvious how he got his name. Before I could test my assumptions, he confirmed it, telling me.

"This is why they call me Train. I'm always on time and never miss a stop!" We both laughed.

Impressed with the amount of money he was picking up out of the streets and knowing he was probably making at least ten times as much money than he was making on his job in a factory I couldn't help but ask why he was still working a job like that.

"This is my hustle money! I've been on my job for twenty years and never missed a day! My job pays the bills and covers my insurance. You 'gotta' keep a job, man! That's why the police still can't figure me out! I go to work on time every day!"

Thoughts ran through my mind as to the mistakes I made by not getting a job in one of the Detroit car factories, where jobs were in abundance. Somehow I was stuck on stupid in the belief I was going to make enough money in the game and be able to retire in the dope game before the factory worker could do thirty years of a daily routine. But since I didn't want to work in the factory, he let me see that I at least need to have a legitimate business and began working toward one.

The more we talked the more of my questions were answered. My thoughts changed from how the old man got in the dope game to how much cash he was probably sitting on making ten times the money I was making on the same goods. Not using anything himself all of his investment was turned into cash money.

Eventually spilling out the question of asking how much money I had cost him and what I could do for the inconvenience caused, he revealed that his lawyer was a high profile drug lawyer and owed him a favor. He told me I wouldn't have to pay for what had already been done but any future services rendered to me were my responsibility.

We talked and rode around for much of the evening until the last stop was to drop me off at Deb's. I had the rest of the night to be free. I knew what was about to happen in court the next morning and that there was a possibility of having to stay in the state until the case was over. There was even the possibility of having to do time in an out of state jail. He dropped me off and I later retired to my strange bed in a strange town.

The next morning Debbie took me took the courthouse, meeting with the attorney before my docket was called. After hearing the case the judge ruled that I should be prosecuted in the state where the actual crime was committed. I was free to go home, but it was inevitable that the police were going to come knocking one day soon after getting there. There was no bail and no warrant, yet. The only hope was that the insurance company would be happy getting the car back in perfect condition and wouldn't press charges.

I didn't waste any time booking a flight back to Detroit. Still holding all my money, I had enough to buy a ticket and was going home with enough to keep the business going for a week or so if something could be found. Carrying a package back with me to Detroit was too risky now that the police knew I was probably there in New York on a drug related deal in the first place. I waited for Train to get home from work to drive me to the nearest airport, which was in Buffalo, less than an hour away. I paid for my ticket, got on the plane and took my dumb ass back to Detroit.

* * *

The one-hour flight didn't give me much time to think about all the self-imposed idiocy brought on with immaturity and a drug habit. The thoughts running through my mind set in motion the chills running through my bones from withdrawal symptoms. Embarrassed by no longer having the new ride I told everyone I just bought left me with figuring out my next lie.

Not only having caused havoc in Train's and my world, I would also have to give Leonard the heads up that the police might be contacting him. The car was one thing but the way he got me the paperwork through the DMV might involve the person who prepared the phony documents, which could cause them to lose their job as well. I suddenly became asshole of the decade.

When the plane landed I took a cab home. Without luggage to claim, I was reminded why the Customs officer pulled me over and started the whole mess. The few times I had flown in the past there was always some type of bag. This time I made the trip back home naked, walking, and empty-handed.

When the taxi hit Gladstone the agony increased riding down the darkened street. It was the first time in a long while being in the back of a cab going home. When riding cabs I usually had a car parked in front of the house. Beverly and the kids were happy to see me after my tribulation. Though I had lost much, I still had a home and a bed, and I promptly went to sleep in them.

When I woke the next day the reality was setting in and I looked ahead. My focus now was to get some dope to sell and buy another car. I called Leonard and wired him up on what had happened and that chances were the police would be contacting us soon. My apology for my stupid mistake was all I had but not enough to ensure our long-term friendship would continue.

I still had enough money to start looking for another ride, needing to keep at least several hundred bucks to get a package to get back to rolling, but a car was something that could be had cheap in the Motor City. Looking through the local auto trader magazine I found someone selling a Ford for only three hundred dollars. Seeing the car I couldn't believe my luck. The car was a four door LTD Brougham that had low miles and was clean as a pin. The sellers told me their father who had just passed had owned the car and they just wanted to get rid of it. I paid them the money they asked and drove away. While the car wasn't my style, it was like new. Everything worked including the air conditioning and all the power windows. I had wheels. All I needed was to get back to work.

I started an all out search trying find a consistent connection that would allow me to supply my people and myself with some quality powder without running out every week or two. I made phone calls day and night in hope of making some type of connection with the right people. Every time the phone rang I hoped it was someone on the other end that had scouted me a source. Finally one of my customers informed me he had one. He said he would call me back when he could arrange a meeting, leaving me anticipating his call.

The phone rang.

When answering there was a white man's voice on the other end of the line asking for me by my legal name. My time had come to deal with the car. It was the Livonia Police, telling me they needed me to make a statement as to the circumstances surrounding the vehicle. It would be best to visit them before they came to me so I went to talk, knowing they wouldn't get much information from me either way.

I called Leonard to tell him what was going on but he was a step ahead already because they had called him. I let him know I wasn't going to incriminate him and whatever went down I wasn't going to talk.

I answered to a detective, who began the routine questioning asking me about the car, Leonard, how I wound up with the car, and my role in the insurance fraud. Acting dumber than I was during my recent trip, refusing to give any information. The officer brought in his boss to intensify the questioning to little avail.

Their questioning was plain. They wanted me to turn state's evidence on my partner in crime and leave him holding the bag by himself, though I was just as guilty. It was the legitimate label of being a snitch, something I wasn't about to be. Once the senior officer saw their words didn't move me, in frustration, he unsympathetically stated to the junior cop,

"Charge them both!"

It was something expected and something I prepared myself for. This time I wasn't planning on suffering withdrawals like a few weeks earlier. Before going to the cops I took one of my shoes and removed the leather off the heel and drilled a one-inch round hole and filled it with enough powder to last two to three days. I glued the heel back over the hole leaving no trace. Just as I figured, when booked and searched they never checked the shoe. Incarceration now became a short-term vacation.

The next day I was arraigned and given a personal bond because I'd proven I wasn't a flight risk. I came back to the state knowing it was a possibility of being charged, and also turned myself in without a warrant having to be issued. Once the judge finished I was free to go, at least until the outcome of the case.

When it went to trial I was given a two-year probation, a slightly stiffer sentence than the first case with the gun.

Now charged with conspiracy to commit fraud I had my second stamp of disapproval. One more case now and I would be seen as an habitual criminal and be certain to do time if ever busted again for any felony charge. My chances of having the first case expunged were now thrown out the window for life because the law only allowed for one felony being removed from the record after the case was five years old. There would be no forgiveness from society from that point, no probability of a good job one day once I woke up, no need to ever apply for a gun permit to protect myself and family; no need to stop selling dope.

CHAPTER 8: THE DRIVE-BY

Though able to hold my clientele together with hither and thither offered through middlemen, it forced me to be inconsistent in product quality, leaving me in a constant hunt for better dope. A customer of mine, Larry, whom I met since starting my own business, learned of my need to make a contact with a good supplier who could hold a sack long enough that would allow me to grow from consistency. Larry told me about a guy he knew who had been one of the major rollers in the 'hood before getting knocked. He'd just gotten out of lockup and was trying to rekindle his business. He took me to and introduced me to Herbert, a small framed, dark-skinned brother who didn't look like he lifted any weights or exercised much while he was in lock up like most, but looked more like a small framed Ethiopian. He needed a clientele as well that bought the kind of small weight I was looking for, which would allow him to handle larger pieces.

We met in various places throughout the city until he felt comfortable dealing with me. Once he confided in me we met at an apartment. From there, we became more like friends – learning as much about me as I knew about him. He revealed to me that before he got busted he had some of the best product available in the city and that he had more than a half million dollars on his bed a week before he got cracked.

Herbert and me did business for over a year until he got pressured by his future wife to get out of the game. It was a shock to me and I could take it no other way than he must have been madly in love or maybe just tired. It hadn't been that long since he started and too soon to reap any benefits from his efforts. He had just bought another new car and seemed to be doing well but he didn't have enough money to quit. I didn't complain though; he gave me his supplier, his brother, Joe.

The first time doing business with Joe was like hitting the jackpot. Not only did he not mind bringing me what I wanted, which lessened my chances of getting caught in the street, but the package he brought gave me almost twice as much as what I paid for. He didn't use drugs and acted like what he was carrying around was only what it looked like, powder. To make it better, he didn't care. Not only was there always more in the package than paid for, it was top quality to the point the medicine in it could be smelled when the cover foil was opened. The quality allowed me to cut it and still have something that would tempt people I hadn't seen in a long time.

Joe's generosity paid well. He was steady, prompt, and always gave me more than what I ordered. My little change started adding up as my profits tripled. The flat I lived in became too busy because the kids were there most of the time. It was where they lived and too much traffic was adding the feeling of them being raised in a drug house or living in danger, a little different than just having a few of the same people frequenting. It never should have gone that far but I couldn't afford two places.

The drugs also seemed to get the better of my squeeze, Bev. Just like most others on drugs, idleness consumed her life as the drugs took control. I wanted to get them away from her but the problem was that she had a habit and would have to leave her with one, which was the hardest part. I was partially the reason of her having a habit because I fed it so long. While there were many reasons to be found and questions to be answered, the decision was to add some division between her, the kids and the drugs. In the end, the decision to move my business and myself to a new location became of most importance.

I found an apartment on a street called Burlingame, about three miles away from the place I'd come to know as my home. Now in a strange territory, it was still the chance to be alone long enough to think about what to do with my life that was moving in a circle. I'd saved a few dollars and had paid off the Probation Department for the conspiracy to fraud charge. I was free because all they wanted was the money. I now had a renewed sense of freedom and the chance to start a new episode of my life.

Joe didn't mind the move either; he continued to bring my packages to the new spot. The move also allowed me freedom to fill some fantasies because my product lured both male and female. It didn't take long to set up shop on my first floor apartment furnished with a stove and a refrigerator. I bought furniture from an outlet store, pots, pans and kitchen utensils to cook with. I even bought a motorcycle to ride like the one I had wanted for years, ever since me and Norman had started riding when we bought bikes some years earlier, keeping it in Nan's garage.

The move gave me a great sense of freedom. Like the one I had for years of being by myself and not attached to one woman in particular. Like most other times though, I was able to get what I wanted when I wanted it. Now, getting not only what I wanted and whom I wanted, I began to get closer to a few of my female customers who could be trusted enough to go to sleep with at night. The drug was my hook, the women were fish, and I had all the bait needed to catch all wanted.

* * *

Out shopping for groceries one day I ran into my old friend Eldon's girlfriend, Paulette. She told me they had gotten married and were doing well. I hadn't seen him in years. I gave her my phone number for him to call me. We had virtually become strangers after Theodore's death. We talked for a while about how our old friends from the 'hood were doing. She promised me she would have Eldon call me when she got home.

Paulette and me checked out of the store at the same time. I walked her to her car to help her with her bags, while making sure she was safe. Her ride was a shiny Oldsmobile Ninety-Eight, a beautiful tan color and looked like they had bought it new. I was even more anxious to talk to my homie from yesteryear to see what he was up to. It didn't take much to figure out he had made his mark in the game.

Eldon called me within an hour after leaving Paulette at the market. We only said a few words to each other before he asked me where I was. After telling him, within a half-hour my doorbell was ringing. I rang him in and opened the door to my first floor apartment to look down the long hall to only see a tall slender figure. Calling out to get his attention, he started walking my way. The darkness of the hall and the wide brim of the gangster hat on his head shadowed a face I hadn't seen in years. Soon as he got close enough for me to see his smile I could see he was wrapped in suede and leather that was the color of Paulette's car.

"Sonny Woods!" he said, as his smile became a grin.

We greeted each other with hugs and embraces. It was like seeing an old war buddy the first time since battle. What was so different now was the way he was adorned. He sported a suede three quarter length blazer, brown slacks that were tucked in brown leather boots and a brown sweater that matched his slacks. He still had his six-inch Afro that bushed below the brim of a fedora that gave home to a striking red feather. It was obvious he had found his way into the dope game like so many of us who were impressed by fast money and far fetched dreams.

It didn't take long for him to confirm my intuitions. While it was discovered I had been rolling long before he got in the game, he had acquired one of the most important things we all saw as a priority, a new ride. We touched base on the things that had been happening in each other's lives over the past years. It was certain now that we would keep in touch. While he had made enough money to afford a down payment on a new life, he was also in need of a good connection to supply the customers who were keeping him afloat. I had the better source and the opportunity to push some larger packages and do it with someone I could trust.

* * *

Money was coming in faster than I could spend it for a while. Eldon and me had gotten to the point we saw each other at least a couple times a week. We had our own little parties on Fridays and got high on the drugs we were selling. I had become quite used to my bachelor apartment in only a matter of a couple months. All my customers were aware of the new spot and came there to make their purchases. The freedom allowed me the chance to cultivate some whorish ways that made living as a bachelor the life of a king. Some of the ladies who had only been customers became bed buddies and pleasure seekers. It was the first time in my life that women seemed happy to take a place in line to spend the night and get high for free. My money slowly stacked and I could finally see the probability of saving a few dollars.

One day I put a wad of cash in my pants pocket and tossed them on the chair in the front of the apartment. I later forgot about the money because of not needing it at the time. One of my customers named Claude came by who was brother to the father of one of Beverly's kids. He usually visited me on his Friday payday. While he was there I made a brief disappearance to get his package from my bedroom in the rear of the apartment. He got his package and left after staying only a few minutes.

Within a few minutes of him leaving I noticed my pair of pants on the chair, remembering leaving over five hundred dollars in the pocket. My first instinct was to check the pockets now that someone had been in the place and close enough to have gone through the pockets. I grabbed up the pants and stuck my hand in the pockets. There was no money in either of the pockets. I'd been ripped off. There was only one person who could have taken it. Claude!

As the adrenaline rush calmed I put my thoughts on getting my cash back. I knew Claude lived in Inkster, which was about fifteen miles from where I lived. Though I knew him enough to trust him as a customer, like most, I didn't know where he lived. The only one who did was the person who introduced me to him, Beverly.

Before making the call to my ex to get the whereabouts of him I called Eldon and told him what had happened and that I might need him to take a ride with me to confront this dude about my paper. He told me he would be available if I needed him. I hung up and called Beverly.

Beverly told me she knew where he lived but didn't remember the address. I told her what had happened with my cash and needed her to show me where he lived. She agreed and told her I would be there in a few so she could show me his house. While she was still a little sour over the break up, she empathized with my loss and promised she would take me to his house.

I picked Bev up within a half hour of hanging up. When I arrived at her house she was ready and seemed happy just to be with me, knowing I would also have something in my pocket I would share with her for sharing her information with me. We rode off and headed southwest toward Inktown. I began to explain to her what had happened and that Claude was my only suspect.

"Are you sure it was him?" she asked.

"It had to have been him. Nobody else had been in the apartment and that close to my pants where the money was!" I told her.

The fall had brought darkness to the early evening hours. We talked for a while until we neared our destination. The small suburb was filled mostly with newer houses that had been built during the late fifties and early sixties. Most of the newly built homes were brick ranch style homes with manicured lawns and quiet streets. When we arrived at Claude's street she directed me to turn. We rode about two blocks down and she told me to slow. When we reached his house she pointed it out to me.

Once having the make on the house and the name of the street we headed back to the city. Bev didn't have much to say during the ride. It seemed that the only thing that was on her mind was our faltered relationship. I made a number of attempts to keep her from thinking about us by making small talk about things irrelevant. In less than a half hour we were back at her place and I dropped her off.

While now knowing where Claude lived, the main focus of thought was how I was going to get my money back. *It's Friday! He probably has already spent my cash or most of it. How will I confront him if he doesn't come to the door once knocking? Of course he'll deny anything and chances are I'm not going to see my money again.*

Back at the apartment I called Eldon. Living only ten minutes away he was ringing my bell shortly. As soon as he entered the apartment he questioned me about what was so important. I shared the robbery story.

"So what you wanna do about it?" he asked, with a smirk.

It was the same question I hadn't been able to answer myself. I told him to hold on a minute. I grabbed my trademark .38 and my coat.

"Come on. We're going to his house and at least cause as much damage as the money he stole. I may not get my money back but I'll make sure he has to spend it for repairs!"

"So what you gon' do?" Eldon asked a second time.

The reality was more evident I wasn't going to see my money again, and now that we were already on our way I had to say something.

"I'm gonna shoot that motherfucker's house up! He's gonna have to use the money he took from me to at least buy some new windows!"

We hit the ditch that was only a couple of blocks away from my place, floating in my three hundred dollar Ford. We talked about Theodore and all the crazy shit we did as kids. Now we had graduated into selling dope thinking we were headed somewhere in a fascination of quick cash and new cars.

We took the route Nan usually took when she drove us to visit our relatives in the newly constructed village near Detroit's Metro Airport. Driving twenty minutes, we exited the freeway at Ecorse Road and took it over to Van Born. When I made the left turn I realized show time was only a few minutes away. Being the main character on stage the anxiety set in. Though I was living a reputation driven lifestyle, shooting up someone's house was not the way Nan had raised me to be but my rage required it.

When we arrived I pointed out the house to Eldon. We drove a block over and parked and walked back to the house on the poorly lit street. It was excellent because the darkness helped hide us.

When we closed with the target house we could see it was dark as if everyone was asleep or not at home. As soon as we got a house away out came the four inch barreled pistol that had lost its stainless burnishing in the darkness. I hesitated to pull the trigger a second and in my haste Eldon snatched the pistol out of my hand and began pulling the trigger.

"This is how you do it!" Like it was something he had done before or someone always wanting to do it.

The flashes of exploding gunpowder out of the barrel lit the dark of night every time he pulled the trigger, emptying the six shot revolver. He didn't seem to be in a hurry as he took his time taking aim.

We didn't run but hurried from the area. Before any neighbors would have made it to look out their windows we were already out of sight. We made it back to the car, put the still warm pistol in a Crown Royal bag, stuffed it in the trunk and drove off.

No sooner than we left I began thinking about how deadly that act of fury could have been. Someone in the house who didn't even know what was going on could have been hit by one of those bullets. *What if one of those bullets really hit someone? I really couldn't tell if he fired high or low. I hope he didn't have any kids in the house!* With all the additional questions I asked myself all night, now I had more, wondering if there was anyone at home and in the line of fire.

By the time we made it back to the freeway the consternation ceased, leaving me to realize that after all I had done and the chances I took failed to produce any of my money. *What if he didn't take it? He did though. Friday night. He's probably out getting high with it, and if he is, he probably has already spent half of it show boating. Shit, he still won't know I was paying him back unless I call him and tell I did it and threaten him to return the rest of my cheddar before something else happens.*

We made it back to the apartment in a short time. There were only two traffic lights between the entrance ramp to the freeway where we got on to the front door of my apartment building. I parked the car and we went in.

Once inside we chuckled about the payback. I still had a feeling that what I had done was dangerous and whether or not someone may have gotten hit with one of those bullets. Eldon must have felt my uneasiness when I first pulled the gun.

"You acted like you was scared to pull the trigger!" he said, looking right through me.

"Nigga I wasn't scared! You snatched the gun out my hand before I had a chance!"

"Yeah, right!"

I broke out with some powder for us to catch a buzz and put my mind on something else. We kicked it a few then called it a night.

Several days passed, building a new bank. More than the six hundred dollars lost had been recouped. My stash of dope was low but I still had enough money to keep things going. Joe dropped me off a fresh package and no sooner than he left, the bell rang. The problem was nobody called me and I had a very strict enforcement of calling first. I answered the intercom and asked who is it?

"Wendy!" she answered.

What the fuck does this bitch want? She knows she ain't supposed to come by here without calling!

I buzzed her in and watched her walk the long hall my direction. When she got close enough to hear my words without being overheard I asked, "What are you doing coming here without calling?"

"I just came by to see if you wanted some company!" I knew what she wanted. She wanted to get high.

"That's cool, but you know you have to always call me first before coming by!"

"I don 't have your number!"

Damn, that's right. Whenever she comes by she's with Ben! I know he'd have a fit if he knew she came by here and have me some of the ass he told me he ain't never got. All the money he done spent getting her high and she ain't never gave up that ass!

"I'll give you my number, but what's up?"

"I figured you might have needed someone to straighten up for you or something." The something was a more attractive proposition than cleaning the house, but I didn't know her enough to let her lay up with me. She was the fire in Ben's eyes and he would do anything to get her naked in a bed. Her caramel brown skin was a shade darker than white chocolate. She wasn't the nicest looking of those in the past, but was good-looking enough to make a guy chase her, namely Ben. He was one of my best customers and I didn't want to lose him over a piece of ass that may have not been worth the time of day.

I invited her to stay for a minute, wanting to see what was really on her mind.

"I guess you can help me clean up...or something!" I told her.

Shy and wide-eyed she said,

"Can you take me home if I stay?"

I didn't ask for all of this shit! She ain't my woman or no shit like that! I don't need my house cleaned up that bad but the idea of the "something" on another day might work!

With cheap gas and padded pockets I went along with it.

"Yeah, I'll take you home. Besides, I haven't been out in almost two days," I told her.

"Ok. I'll tell my sister I have a ride. I'll be right back!"

I must have something she wants and it can't be to clean my house! My place is always straight for the most part. She wants to get high! That's why a nigga ain't supposed to be getting' his woman high. If she gets a habit she winds up on the dope man's lap. And I'll probably let her on mine too!

When Wendy returned I invited her to have a seat and showed her my hospitality with some powder that she probably came for in the first instance. We talked for a few and watched soap operas on television for over an hour before she started her little work detail. She cleaned the kitchen first while I sat. While cleaning the living room she grabbed the pair of jeans that had the missing money.

"What do you want to do with these?"

"Give them to me. I have some more jeans in the back and they need to go to the cleaners."

Going through the empty pockets once again to make sure there was nothing in them, I went to look for the other pair in the bedroom. I did the same routine with them and when sticking my hand in the pocket my knuckles felt an obstruction. It was money and a lot of it. When removing it from the pocket and looking at it my stomach swallowed me. I didn't have to count it to know it was the money I thought Claude took.

Oh shit! I done went and shot this man's house up! Damn, he didn't take it.

Feeling like the fool of the century, my thoughts quickly changed to visions; the mental picture of me in a scene of being the most embarrassed fool in the world. I knew the only way to rectify it was to make it good and give him the wad of money I'd accused him of taking so he could put it toward repairs of his house. Calling to admit it though would take a man and also prove my manhood and integrity. There was nothing else to do but man up and face the music. I called Claude and explained why his house was shot up and that it was me that did it. Telling me that he was wondering what had happened he seemed to take it better than expected. Once telling him I had some money to give him, he came by without haste.

I apologized sincerely about my terrible mistake, gave him the money and a package like he usually bought and hoped it would be enough to make the repairs. He didn't question it, but took the money like it was a gift and after sharing a blow with him, left.

* * *

About a month later, arising to a sunny morning and a chance to get out, I cleaned up and put on some clothes to make runs. I locked up everything and proceeded out the building walking towards where I was parked. Before reaching the sidewalk I noticed my car was gone. *Goddamn! Somebody done got my ass.* The feeling of payback from stealing cars over ten years prior, a Ford for a Ford took over. Though stealing cars was in my past, I had never been paid back for the ones stolen. The heartbreak from my car gone was deepened by the idea of having to walk.

Having the bike only a short distance away, getting to it and leaving it parked overnight at the same place was out of the question. Nan's words echoed in my mind. She always told me that if I took something from someone I'd lose it double, and if someone took something from me I would regain it tenfold. The bitter pill was swallowed, taking the punishment short of a smile.

The only way to possibly get my car back was by calling the police. I made a report and prayed it would soon be found. A couple of days later the police found it on the east side, but without the rear-seat. Everything else was intact except for the steering column, which had damage to the ignition switch. However, I was able to drive it home. Yet having my car back, it seemed like something was still missing.

Several weeks passed and I hadn't seen or heard from Eldon, which was unusual. I went to the apartment where he'd been staying with Paulette. His car wasn't in the parking lot so I didn't try to get in. I figured I'd just go back later and see if he'd made it back home.

When I returned hours later his car was there. Figuring he was just taking a break from everything for a minute I rung his bell. Paulette answered the door.

Instead of Eldon answering the door, all I saw was a woman who looked as if she'd lost her best friend. I knew Eldon couldn't be dead or anything because I hadn't heard anything from anyone else. Upon asking where my homie was she told me he was in the hospital. He had been shot in the face by a cop. Worst part of the news was that he was trying to rob a guy who turned out to be an off-duty police officer.

Damn! What the hell did he do something like that for? I know his habit couldn't have been that bad! He knows he could have come to me to get what he needed!

"How's he doing?" I asked.

"He'll be alright they say. He's in custody of the police. It doesn't look like he'll be out of this one anytime soon though."

Why didn't he call me? Now he's going to jail behind some dumb shit like this!

Realizing I'd lost contact with the closest friend I had at the time I began feeling the emptiness felt when Theodore got killed in the robbery attempt. Now it was Eldon robbing someone else. I told Paulette to make sure she keeps me informed of what was going on with him and left and went back home. On the way, it seemed like I was losing all the friends had and grew up with.

* * *

My run with Joe lasted for nearly a year before things turned in another direction. His product suppliers took a break from the business for while, forcing me back to a life of instability and uncertainty. When my living expenses and the cost of my habit were more than my income I wound up moving out of my apartment and in with my old friend Charles, who had also taken quite a setback and had lost all of his connects. Now he was living the life of a has-been pimp with a habit, but was still the person that would give anyone the shirt off his back.

Charles was still a player though; now running return scams at a department store through one of his ex hoes who fingered a job there. She had a job in the Returns Department and manipulated receipts and refunded the transaction in cash. I helped earn my keep by playing the role of the customer, taking the receipt to her window for a refund. Every time I went I walked away with hundreds. While not having a job at the time my only income was an unemployment check.

My love for opiates left me with both a heroin and methadone habit that I battled with for a while. All the mistakes and troubles were key indications I wasn't thinking with my right mind. It was time for a change and time to get out of the world that was leading me nowhere. Having been shot twice, almost losing my life, and almost taking the lives of others left a sentiment of not liking the person I had become.

Kicking my habit and getting away from the life was something more than a notion – at first. Counselors at the clinic where I was getting my methadone had always told me the withdrawals as well as the habit were all in my mind. Having used hard drugs for almost ten years left me with a gorilla as opposed to a monkey on my back. Every time in the past I didn't have the dog food at my side I suffered withdrawals of two addictions.

Over the period of using both opiates their contradictions began taking a toll on my health. Forced to take the methadone from not having the real thing at hand left me with a routine kidney pain every time I took the cheap substitute. Caught in a catch 22 situation; I was damned if I took it and damned if I didn't. Frustration tormented me. I was sick of the drugs, sick of the guns, sick of making bad mistakes.

One Saturday after leaving the Methadone clinic, I was overwhelmed with the returning pain in my kidneys after taking the medication. It was so severe I found myself holding on to a street sign on my way to the bus stop a block away from the treatment center. At that point it was time to let it all go. Not having the strength to do it alone in the past, it was time to rely on God.

Making it home to Nan's after the twenty-minute bus ride to the basement was where I spent much of my time when growing up. It was there I could still go for a bit of solace. With all the confirmation classes and all the church I had experienced in my adolescence, it was then I fell to my knees in true earnestness, begging God the Father to help me get over my addiction and find a new way of life. I asked Him to help me get over the pain, and asked Him to give me back the years the drugs had taken from my life.

The one thing never abandoned in my life was my relationship with God – Father Mind. He believed in me as I believed in Him. He assured me He would help me and give me the years back if I made the promise never to go back to the stuff that was killing me. Not only did He give me the years back, I walked away from it all without one day of withdrawal. The words of those counselors turned true that it was all in my head.

God is Good....God *is* Mind!

CHAPTER 9: THE MOTORCYCLE CLUB

By the summer of '79, after walking away from my past life and moving back with Nan, I passed much of my time riding the bike I had stored in her garage. It was the one thing to show for all the years of waste. The bike was a red 750cc Honda that had an eight inch extension on it and lowering blocks that gave it a chopper like profile without altering the frame, allowing the bike to still maintain controllability. It had a custom king queen seat; a hog wheel with lowering blocks that dropped the rear end closer to the ground and heart shaped rear view mirrors.

Taking a cruise alone on the bike, stopping at a traffic light, a guy pulled up next to me riding a black Kawasaki as I waited for the light to change green. He asked me where I was headed. Speaking over the loud noises of the mufflers of both bikes.

"Nowhere, just riding."

"Want to take a ride?" he asked.

I actually was out wasting time anyway so he was really on time.

"Sure, why not!"

"Come on! Let's go this way"

We changed the course from going straight down Twelfth, turned right on Webb, and shot over two blocks to the John C. Lodge Freeway and hit the ditch, heading north. Arriving at the Davison freeway interchange we took it east.

As we rode I set focus on the black biker leather, patches and trinkets attached to his vest. He wore chaps with fringes and motorcycle club colors in the center of his back. The name "Big Joe" was embroidered on a separate patch worn above the other patches with the club's name; Elegant Disciples. I'd never known anyone in a motorcycle club or had even been to one. Big Joe seemed to be pretty cool though, and I didn't feel threatened so I opened up the throttle and rode as hard as he did.

We rode only about three or four miles before we exited the freeway. We took the service drive on the Davison freeway and made a left turn that took us over the same, turned left again. Soon we arrived at a small storefront building painted red with black trim and had a painted insignia like the face of the center patch on the colors Big Joe wore. The letters converged over the top of the skeleton's top hat on its head, which wore a monocle and spelled out the words "Elegant Disciples" M/C. We backed up to the curb and turned the bikes off. Big Joe asked, "What's your name?"

"Al," I answered.

"Al Capone!"

A big smile lit his face as if he knew me or had the name ready and waiting.

"Come on inside. Let me show you my clubhouse and introduce you to some of my brothers. I'll buy you a beer!" he said.

We walked into the dimly lit remnant of what appeared to once be a store or some other type of business. There was a pool table in the middle of the floor and a jukebox that stood lonesome in the corner. The records that played from the old

Wurlitzer catered to the Blues and the first recordings of what some would call Hip-Hop. And like most jukes back then, a quarter would get you three selections, while a half dollar would get you seven.

I ordered a Budweiser while I began admiring the ten to sixteen foot trophies that hung from the ceiling because they were too tall to stand on the floor. I got curious and asked Big Joe about the history of the awards.

He explained that the club won the trophies from other clubs for having the most members during cabarets or other events where members from other clubs attend. These events were held to show solidarity and support for the club allies. Some of the trophies were for traveling the longest distance and some for best-dressed rider, best-dressed club, longest distance rider, and other awards. Most of them came from out of town. It was enough to show me that there was more to the motorcycle clubs than just partying and catching a buzz. I became interested in learning more. It seemed it could be the remedy for changing environments; something needed to leave behind the world I'd left.

"The name "Al Capone" was one I could see myself wearing. It was a form of identification in the biker world where everyone lived with aliases that related to something big or dangerous. The name kind of fitted me because of my interest in mafia movies and lifestyles, the life of the notable in particular. I admired the gangsters solely for their loyalty and dedication to their families and entrusted confidants.

* * *

It didn't take much time for me to decide to join the club. It was something that could fill a void and something that would take my attention from the life I was leaving behind. It didn't take long for my name to take root. Little did Big Joe know, the name was perfect for me; not because I tried to act like a gangster, but the flamboyance and idealism associated with the noted figure were simpatico with my thinking and lifestyle.

One of my newfound brothers was "Ice Man." He was like the mascot of the club, and the only one who actually lived in the clubhouse. Since he knew the history of the motorcycle club world, he was the one who introduced me to most of the people. While things, as I'd begun to see them, were relatively peaceful among clubs, Ice Man told me of one club they always had trouble with and that I should always be on the lookout for the members of a club called *"Satan's Sidekicks."*

While the change of environments was needed, I hadn't contemplated the situation of possibly being drawn into a shootout. Ice told me the Sidekicks hated us with a passion because there was rumor that the president of my club killed their president during a shootout after crashing another club's party. The best thing he told me was that they didn't come to our club to party. Nevertheless, with the reputation they had, vengeance was to be had if they really believed we killed their president. I learned rumor had it they did, and it was only a matter of time before there would be trouble coming my way.

Nevertheless, I went ahead and enjoyed the biker world and my new clubhouse. Though it wasn't close to being ritzy in the slightest, it was like a home away from home. After being initiated and receiving my full set of patches (colors), I convinced the body of members to get rid of the juke box and let me build a D.J. booth so we could play our own music on our Thursday night party, which in turn would generate thirstier dancers and people who would buy more drinks, hence, creating more revenue. I changed all the lighting, added a disco ball to the ceiling, installed new speakers, amplifier, duo turntables and the works, including the microphone. The idea worked, and as my D.J. skills increased my popularity took off like a rocket. At the time, we were the only club to have a disc jockey on a party night. From that point, anything I said seemed gospel.

While having some influence on my president, and on some of the members, the next thing to do was convince them they need to have a shotgun in the booth where I played and one behind the bar on party night in case anything might happen. The proximity of the booth gave me an overall and clear view of anything that came through the door or jumped off in the building. That time everybody didn't buy my idea because of the cost of the guns.

We continued our party on Thursday as always. The influence of our new sound system generated more and more partygoers. A few of the clubs noticed our increase of business and the enjoyment of the new aura. They began to follow suit, focusing on generating an increase in their revenue.

The club's party became more like a night of business. Instead of all partying, it was our night to make money. Our income tripled in only a matter of several months. It was kind of like a move that Capone would make: pull them in, give them what they want, and make a profit from it!

CHAPTER 10: GANG WAR

I was just getting warmed up playing music one Thursday night when some bikers came through the door. They were all unfamiliar faces. Though I didn't know everyone in the biker clique, most of those who frequented our spot came through routinely, giving me the chance to get to know them and their patches. Nevertheless, if they got in the door I figured they must have been all right. One rule of thumb that was always followed: search everybody that doesn't wear colors; the threat was they had colors on and not subject to search. I continued to file through a stack of records to find my next hour of selections.

When moving around in the tight booth someone pushed the small door in. I looked up into some dude's face and he was high. He looked spaced out in another time zone. But now he was in the wrong place. He took his hand, reached past me and stopped the turntable playing the music, telling me he wanted to play. I pushed him back out the booth. When he turned his back towards me I saw an unfamiliar looking insignia of a figure wearing an Afro with a pitchfork and riding a motorcycle. The top rocker of the patches read "Satan's Sidekicks."

The day Ice Man warned me about seemed to have come early. The shotgun I urged the club to buy was suddenly confirming its importance. While the one who pushed the door in on me carried a chain, his actions were as if he had more weapons than we did in the whole club; I just didn't know what their motive was. But for the moment, I didn't know what was about to happen.

While the "Kicks" didn't do any major damage that night they could have. Not to my surprise, in the next club meeting everyone suggested we should get ourselves armed. Though the heat was off for the moment, Ice Man exclaimed,

"They will be back!"

At that point figuring out what it was I'd truly gotten myself into was the only thought that came to mind. It wasn't that of being scared to fight, but I'd already come close to losing my life and hadn't completely healed from the wounds of the first near fatal gunshot almost ten years earlier. I just couldn't see getting myself into a war that had started long before my coming on the scene. On the other hand, it wasn't about quitting either; that's what was sought out in the probationary period, to see where my heart truly was and whether or not I was a quitter. I had already proven myself to be dedicated. As a matter of fact, some had begun to look to me for leadership. It would have been like cowardice to leave at the first sign of trouble.

Months passed before we heard from the Sidekicks again. We continued doing what we did while they terrorized many of the small clubs by literally taking motorcycles from the members as they watched. Sometimes they even took the colors right off the backs of some bikers, with no retaliation. Many bikers who had taken part in what was known as "The Association" were primary targets of the Sidekicks. Most of the clubs were in attendance when the shootout occurred that killed their leader at the clubhouse of the US Enterprise during an association party. They compared themselves to outlaws, while the members of the Association were viewed by the Kicks as bourgeois civilians wearing colors. My club just happened to be in the patronage of those un-liked.

* * *

As time went on the Kicks continued to harass a few of the clubs in the city that were seen as weak, or tacky because of the way some clubs displayed what the Kicks considered uncool behavior. The rumor that our president killed theirs only grew, stirring the pot for revenge.

In the heat of an oncoming war, the Sidekicks drew first blood by coercing their women, their property, to take the colors off the back of one of our women members when she was caught out in the street wearing her patches. This action was probably intended to also display contempt for our social-like club that allowed women to be members opposing the outlaw's belief that women shouldn't be members, only the *property* of a male biker of the club who acts as their sponsor.

The decision of what to do about regaining our colors was serious. Talk was going around town that one of the Kicks was wearing the centerpiece upside down on the seat of his pants. This type of action among bikers would be seen as a total disrespect of that club. Nevertheless, we didn't want trouble, and I didn't want to be a soldier in a war. It had only been two years prior leaving hell. I was more than happy to see my leader hesitate to make a move on a club that probably outgunned us ten to one.

A few weeks after we heard we were being dissed we got a call from one of our females in the club while we were in a meeting. She told us that her colors had also been taken. Obviously, the fact was becoming evident that we were being pushed into a corner. We had to make a decision - one we knew could wind up costing lives. We were becoming outlaws, forced into a choice of a shootout or to leave town. We knew we had to get our colors back and the only way was by reversing the policy of taking colors, theirs for ours. What we didn't know was that we were about to be participants in one of the most vicious and deadly motorcycle-club wars in the history of Detroit.

The next decision was that of being the aggressors. We learned they were having a party on that same night. We figured the Sidekicks would never expect an attack from us, less much on their own turf, so we gathered all the weapons we could get our hands on and filled three vehicles with shotguns and Elegant Disciples and went after our goods for bargaining.

Getting caught in a car filled with illegal firearms driving across town was among the first of thoughts that ran through my mind. Getting shot was the main one. The last thing I wanted to do was to repeat the episode of getting more of my organs cut out. This time I might no be as lucky as the first. When joining the club I never expected walking into a feud like one seen on television. But it was too late to walk out. Not only had I filled one of the offices of the club, some might have seen me as the leader of this low-budget suspense drama with real characters and real bullets.

We left our clubhouse, hit the Davison, then the Lodge freeway and drove about seven miles west to our destination at Puritan and Meyers. When we got less than a block away from the Kick's clubhouse we got our of our cars, got our guns from the trunks, went over our plan one last time. This was to ride up in front of the clubhouse with a van and a car and place another car at a location for escape in case things didn't go as planned. Our plan was to cover all entrances so no one would come out shooting, which would put their visitors in harms way. All of them being outlaws, including their guests, we knew if thing didn't go right we could be in war with the toughest outlaw clubs in the city like the Hell Lovers, Sin City Disciples and the Outcast who were at the party that night. We couldn't screw up.

We moved out of the cars toward their house. There were thirteen of us when we got there and we hoped there would be thirteen when we left. We had to make sure we went home with everybody. It was clear that we would not to fire a gun unless it was absolutely necessary. We figured if someone starting shooting it could end up in a full-fledged shoot out because many of the bikers were known for being strapped. More than likely the Kicks would have starting shooting first, so our mission was to surprise them and get the drop before anyone had a chance.

As we neared the corner of the club it was clear to see we had the element of surprise in our favor. There were only about ten people standing on the sidewalk, where at most times during a party in the summer the sidewalk would be overflowing. Our plan was to take the colors off somebody's back, something we knew that would not be accepted very well. I knew once we made our move we would start a war unlike anything I had ever been involved in. The sweat in the palms of my hands began building, as did the adrenaline in my body as we approached the clubhouse.

We made our move.

When we got in front of the clubhouse a couple of Kicks were sitting of their motorcycles less than ten feet away from where we stopped. It first appeared our task would be easy and without gunfire. The van stopped. My heart began beating faster as the door opened.

"Don't move. On your knees!"

It was so sudden nobody had time to think less much draw a gun. The visitors standing in front on the sidewalk were stunned. Not only did they not know what was going on, someone was making a move in front of their eyes they couldn't believe.

"All we want are these colors on your backs!" someone yelled.

As the one closest to the street was suddenly held at gunpoint, he was forced to remove his colors. The other Sidekick within reach knew he was next when the expressions on his face changed. When forced to remove his from his back, we heard a couple of shots coming from the rear of the building, meaning someone was trying to come out of the back door which was covered by only handguns. We knew our time was running out. The one thing started that we didn't want, gunfire. It was time to move fast. Those covering us at the front of the building were placed across the street.

As we got back into our van gunshots rang out from the front. Those who covered the back were overwhelmed. After they left covering the rear, the Kicks hurriedly made it out the back door and up onto the roof and across the building to the front. Once there they began to fire at us out front. As we tried to return to our vehicles to leave, the fire increased. With the speed born of desperation we were gone, not knowing if everyone made it away safely or if anyone had been shot. It would only be known once all the vehicles made it back to our house and a count was taken.

It was unbelievable everything went so well. We didn't see anyone of us shot so we assumed we had all gotten away safely. Until that moment I had never seen a set of Sidekick colors that close. As the idea came to my mind to look closer at the teddy bear looking devil riding a motorcycle up close, I couldn't help but notice though that not only had we taken Sidekick colors, the bottom rocker on one of the sets read Toledo, instead of Detroit. Not only did we now have the Detroit gang wanting our heads now, but also their brothers from Toledo, Ohio, home of the well known "Black Moses." Nobody had to tell us that stepping on the feet of Moses would lead to things escalating.

On our way back to the clubhouse I felt a sense of victory. Our mission was temporarily over but the adrenaline continued to flow. I couldn't help but to think how angry the Kicks would have to be. Nobody in the city would have believed an inferior club like the Elegant Disciples would have taken on the infamous Satan's Sidekicks.

After discovering everyone had made it back safely we begin to critique the raid. The most frightening of stories came from one of my brothers who was one of those covering our backs stationed across the street in an abandoned lot. He told us that when the Kicks started shooting at them across the street his hat was shot off his head, claiming he could feel the heat of the bullet streak across the top of his skull. The story sounded like he was exaggerating a bit, but he sure didn't have his cap anymore.

Though it seemed we had done our job well and we were victorious in our feat, we knew the battle had just begun. With the reputation the Sidekicks held, nobody had to tell us that it would only be a matter of time before they would be paying us a visit. We knew they would be coming so we got ready.

Figuring we only had probably an hour at most before they would be showing up, we double checked our weapons and, designated a post for everyone to man. We turned off all the lights in front of the club and made sure everyone made it a point not to go out the front door just in case there would be a sniper waiting for an easy pick.

We waited over an hour. Nobody showed. Nevertheless, everyone held their positions, although the prediction of them coming seemed inaccurate. We were almost ready to call it a night when someone on the roof of our clubhouse noticed a suspicious looking van stopping on the service drive across the freeway. There were knocks on the roof signaling us in the club that this was probably what we were waiting for. Everyone got ready to shoot in case the van crossed on the overpass and turned in our direction.

Just as the van turned onto the over pass coming in our direction, the knocks got louder from the roof. Someone hollered,

"That's them!"

We knew if the van made the U-turn and came over the bridge in our direction it would be them. I guessed that by the van stopping on the other side of the freeway there was someone inside with a high-powered rifle waiting for easy picks walking out of the door. The van made the two turns necessary that would position it right in our immediate sights. As it came closer it got so quiet you could hear a mouse pee on a cotton ball.

The van approached and slowed almost to a stop. When it did, it seemed that everyone began to fire at the van. It must have been hit at least fifteen times before the driver got the chance to pull away. While the passenger in the van got off a couple of shots, it was too much firepower for them. They took off.

As the van began to speed away, some kept firing at it. When the van made it to the intersection a block away, a car pulled out of the side street and began chasing after the van. We didn't know who it was and why they suddenly began giving chase.

We would later learn that the yellow car pulling from the side street and giving chase just so happened to be Secret Service agents in the ghetto. Now, not only was their plan to be snipers foiled, they now had government agents after them. They even shot at the agents a few times during the pursuit and were arrested after the chase didn't turn in their favor. Now, we were even more hated than we were in the beginning.

CHAPTER 11: GANG WAR (PT. 2), THE AMBUSH

The following day some of us were in our clubhouse shooting pool and having an informal meeting. We could hear the loud mufflers from a few motorcycles in the distance. At first I figured it was a few of our members coming, but then most of our members who rode bikes were already in the club. The mufflers got louder as they slowed in front of the clubhouse then suddenly pulled away. It was now so loud it called for us to go to the door but with caution.

　When we opened the door the last of the motorcycles were just a few feet away. There must have been at least thirty motorcycles if not more. Before we got the chance to wonder why they came one of my brothers noticed a blue cap in the doorway. It was White Boy's cap, the one he claimed had been shot of his head. He had told the truth. The cap had a bullet hole right in the front of the cap. Whoever shot it off his head must have known they did and saw it. By them dropping off the cap the way they did, the message was clear, there were more bullets to come, and maybe the next one wouldn't miss.

We made it a rule not to go anywhere alone. When one went, everybody went. We were all in it together, and we had to show all the strength we had. It wasn't time to boast or brag but a time to show we weren't the pussies we were thought to be. We had two sets of Sidekick colors in our possession holding them ransom as a tool of leverage to get the dispute dissolved as well as get our colors back. We didn't know what was on their minds and they knew they had to do what we wanted in order to get them back.

Two days later, Tuesday, the third day after we played our wild card we went out to party like nothing had happened. I knew we were walking targets but it was no time to show fear. While the Sidekicks didn't hang out routinely as we did, it was time to keep our eyes wide open. When we showed up at the home of the Detroit Gentlemen's club on Grand River, I could tell everyone knew what had happened by the looks on their faces. The expressions of many were sympathy. Others were surprised to see us out. Before we made it to the entrance of the club, a member of Hell Lovers, asking, approached me.

"Are you ready to die?"

I was caught by surprise and took the offensive.

"Are you ready to kill me?" I asked.

The last thing I needed now was more trouble. It was obvious that the news had spread throughout the motorcycle club circuit and we were the main topic of every discussion. While some bikers were happy to hear what we had done, others knew we had insulted a club that would undoubtedly seek revenge.

The heat in the city began to rise from the Elegant Disciple/Sidekick feud. Rumor had it that the Sidekicks had taken their colors off so they wouldn't be noticed. Being only a new kid on the block with only two years in the club, I only knew a handful of my brothers amongst the hundreds. The only thing I knew to look out for was a biker wearing black jeans with blue jean shorts over them. They were the only ones in the city to wear them like that; it was their trademark.

Nobody had enough nerve to imitate them. If you were a copycat you would be asking for trouble. Everybody knew it, so nobody dared.

The following day, Wednesday, we made our journey to the east side of town – to the home of the Detroit Rams on Kercheval Street. By the time we had a couple of drinks and were enjoying the party, we got a message from someone who answered the phone.

"Someone called and said something's about to happen at your clubhouse!"

I knew whatever it was about, it had to do with the colors we had in our possession. Nevertheless, it was time to make the eight-mile trip back to our clubhouse to see if anything had really happened.

When we got near our clubhouse, which was in open view at a distance. Smoke could be seen rising into the night skies over the building we called home. It was plain they were making good on their warning. When getting closer it didn't appear the place was on fire, but the smoke still had to be explained. After we got in front of the club and got off our motorcycles we could see glass on the ground below the wood paneled façade that covered plate glass windows. The smell of gunpowder lingered in the air. Smoke was still visible in the exterior vestibule. Most significant, twined wire led from the doorway about a hundred feet around the corner and into the street where obviously they were connected to a plunger or detonator. The Kicks were now using explosives and someone was trained to use them.

Nobody had to tell me things were really getting serious. After all my days of surviving using heroin and other elicit drugs, it was quite possible now for me to lose my life on something that got started before I even became a part of the club. Out of over thirty clubs in the city it suddenly seemed I joined the worst one I could have. The only thing I could do was to try to see the value in the patch I had on my back and whether or not it was worth me dying for.

Over the next couple of days the heat rose in the city. Everyone in the club even got closer knowing we were all in this thing together. We continued to watch each other's backs more than ever. We were able to make our position known to the Kicks, which was to return our colors and leave us alone. The Sidekicks made it known they weren't ready to give in to our demands. Our negotiations led nowhere. Either we get this thing resolved or shut down the club completely. The latter wasn't considered. Besides, this time they drew first blood and just like any other club or gang, you never run from the first sign of trouble.

A week passed without any resolution. Things almost seemed to have gotten back to normal as far as us resuming our usual habits of hanging out and having visitors and the open use of our club. Because there was always someone there, friends and neighbors as well as bikers always stopped in so we made it a point to have someone there. Bikers always stopped in to grab a beer, especially in the summer when the weather was right.

That Monday one of my club members had a visit from some young ladies who Big O had invited to the club. They stayed several hours shooting pool and playing pinball enjoying themselves before they decided to leave at about nine 'o clock. Ice Man had got sweet on one them and decided he would ride along with 'O,' giving him a chance to hit on his new infatuation. As everyone was about to walk out the door we began discussing where we would go and party that night. There was one party on the east side and one on the west. We didn't cease to go out and party every night though because it has always been a custom among bikers – a way of supporting one another to pay the expense of having a commercial building. Only now we just had to be a little more cautious because of the ongoing conflict. When we went outside we made it a point to look around for any strange-parked vehicles.

This night was no different. We checked the sidewalks before walking out. Everything was clear. White Boy had a cousin who had recently started coming around spending time after learning he could enjoy himself in the biking circuit. The two of them walked out together. Ice Man got in the back of the van along with the young lady he wanted to talk to. White Boy and Ty walked in front of the van and were talking while I stood on the sidewalk next to the van. By then we decided we would go east to the Boogie Down M/C., which partied every Monday night. As usual, we went to one or both of the two clubs that partied on that night. Just as Big O clicked his seat belt the sound of twenty loud fireworks appearing to be coming from nowhere echoed. I could hear ricochets off Big O's van. White Boy fell forward and then onto the street. His cousin fell next to him.

Ambush! Several snipers shot from the rooftops of the buildings a few doors away with high-powered rifles.

I fell back up against a brick front wall. The shooting stopped as quick as is started. Ice Man was the first to respond, hollering out, "Oh shit, I've been shot!"

I yelled out to Big O.

"Are you all right?"

"I think I've been hit too!" he called.

Before I could check on Big O I couldn't help but notice the young lady in the back with Ice Man through the doors that hadn't yet been closed. I could see eyes roll up in her head as she slumped over. I rushed to the van to help. It was obvious that the bullet that came through the roof of the van struck her in the chest – near her heart. For some reason I knew that she would take her last breath before the ambulance would arrive. Her eyes had the same look my father's did before he took his last breaths.

Ice Man said he'd been shot in the hand.

In a panic I ran back into the clubhouse telling someone to call and ambulance.

"Call 911!" I said.

"Tell them we need two ambulances!"

I went back to check on White Boy. He was laying face down with his cheek on the ground moaning in pain. He had been shot in the back.

"We're getting you an ambulance." I told him.

He begged me, "Get me first Al! Please get me first!"

It was obvious his pain was unbearable. I didn't have to guess how he could have felt. I had a very good idea though I hadn't been shot with a rifle. Being shot is being shot, no matter what kind of gun the bullet comes from.

When I realized it, four out of six of us had been shot. I was the only one standing in open sight who didn't get hit. I could have been face down on the ground dead. The thought of that left me with weak knees and wrecked nerves. There were people lying all around. There had actually been so many bullets riddling through the roof of Big O's van he thought he had been shot but hadn't.

It took about fifteen minutes for the first ambulance to arrive. It seemed like an hour. I knew the young lady who had been shot had taken her last breaths, and even if some miracle happened she wouldn't make it to the hospital alive. When I'd held her in my arms I was holding death. I checked her pulse one last time; she had none.

White Boy got his request to ride in the first ambulance – along with the woman with the fatal wound. Tyrone rode in the second ambulance along with Ice Man. And by the time the third ambulance made it to the scene along with numerous numbers of police cars and detectives, so did the news media. It would interrupt local program broadcasting to report that a war between two rival motorcycle gangs has resulted in the death of at least one person and the wounding of several others.

While it seemed proper to think about revenge, the focus now was on White Boy and his cousin. We figured Tyrone would be all right but White Boy's wounds were obviously much more serious than the other two survivors that had been shot, Ice Man and Tyrone. The police that had showed up on the scene began to question all who were still at the scene. What started as an apparent feud turned into a homicide investigation. Nonetheless, as soon as we were able to shake the interrogation we went to the hospital to check on our comrade struggling for his life.

116 Guns, Drugs, Gangs, and Anger

CHAPTER 12: GANG WAR (PT. 3), A NEW REPUTATION

Paul scheduled a meeting at a place away from our clubhouse. All I knew about was a meeting the motorcycle association had that would take place that day at the Detroit Gentleman's clubhouse. Somehow, I assumed the meeting of the latter was the one and went to that. Traveling alone and wearing my colors wasn't a problem in spite of the unending rivalry as most traveled in groups since the war began.

When I arrived at the meeting I didn't see any of my members, realizing this wasn't the place I was supposed to be at. No one had told me personally about *our* conference at one of the member's house that was taking place at the same time. There were over forty bikers packed into the monthly meeting. The basis of their discussion was about the rivalry between the Elegant Disciples and the Satan's Sidekicks. When they noticed me in the house every one's eyes appeared focused on me.

"You all need to get that shit straightened out!" one of the voices yelled out.

Never thinking much of the socialistic set I wasn't amazed to see that everyone in the meeting acted like they were placing a connection to what they did at their independent clubhouses. Some spoke with a fear that the police would soon be visiting their clubs to see what was going on as opposed to being focused on the assaulting gang. While everyone there had something to say, there wasn't much suggestion of solutions for the problem. One of the bikers at the meeting spoke out that he was roommate with one of the Kicks and suggested he call and arrange a meeting for us to come to a truce. He called and talked to the other side and they approved the meeting, but at their clubhouse. They happened to be at their clubhouse at the time so I left immediately. On the way out the door I heard someone say loudly, "He won't be back!" Followed by laughter.

Being the only member from my club aware of the meeting with the Sidekicks and the one having agreed to attend it, I began the two-mile ride in the T-Bird. Knowing it was dangerous to go alone wasn't enough to make me back out of it. If I came up missing the only way my members would find me would be through the bikers at the meeting I had just left.

By then it would be too late.

I also figured that going alone would show that we weren't as timid as they predicted. My near death experience from being shot and the streets that reared me left me slight of fear. I thought they would have to respect me for having enough nerve to come up in their clubhouse by myself during a war and while having their rags in our possession. They had ours too. And I wanted them back.

The Sidekick clubhouse was on Puritan and Meyers in a small business district on the northwest side of town, a short distance from the Gentlemen's. I drove Hubbell to Puritan, turned right and drove towards an unforeseeable outcome.

Parking across the street from the red clubhouse a few minutes later I exited the car and walked across the street. I rang the doorbell to what seemed like a place where nobody was home. The doorbell could be heard from the outside. A few moments later someone opened the door. The inside appeared dark. That person motioned me inside. There was another Sidekick standing about twelve feet in front of me, wearing the trademark jean shorts over jeans.

"Search him!" a voice hollered out.

"Hold on!" The one opening the door began searching me.

He finished his search.

"Go on back," he told me.

My pupils had not yet adjusted from the glaring sunlight. I walked in the direction that was pointed to in a back room, passing a noose hanging in the front of the doublewide storefront building. Restricted to my peripherals, the only thing that could be certain was that there were about ten shadows standing around a pool table. The light over the table, angling its light down, didn't allow a full description of anyone. Someone who had a larger butcher knife and was stabbing it into the marble tabletop directed,

"I'm Silver Smoke! I'm the president. What do you want?"

Looking at the knife more than anything and thinking about the noose, I replied,

"My name is Capone. I came here with hopes of getting our problem settled."

"What do you want?"

Speaking over the lump in my throat, I replied, "We want our colors back!"

"We don't have them!"

With an answer leaving me without words, I focused more on the knife and the noose. There was yet the question about getting their colors back, and not showing doubt of getting them one way or another. What I did understand though was that it appeared we weren't going to solve the matter with everyone getting what they wanted.

As my eyes allowed me to make out the shadowed faces in the room I noticed one young man who had on a patch over one eye named Mike Dog. Dray, his brother was the one who was known for getting shit started and stealing motorcycles from members in other clubs, and the one who crashed my deejay's booth. Another one of the silhouettes wore a derby, inclusive of biker adornment and almost all of them wore jean shorts over jeans. Some had Sidekick insignias printed on t-shirts and some didn't, but everybody there wore a vest back grounding their colors with devils riding motorcycles in a wheelie.

"You gotta lot of motherfuckin' nerve coming here by yourself! The only reason we don't kill you is because we gotta respect you for coming up in here like that!" Smoke said as a few laughed.

"It's not nerve. Men should always be able to talk!" I replied.

My rubber legs shook with an undetected tremble. A few of them noticeably had been holding in their anger but seemed edgy. I felt like it was better being by myself because they might have been intimidated if there had been someone with me and things probably would have gotten real nasty. I didn't know if it was my last time to see the daylight I was so anxious to be seen again.

"What can we do to get this shit settled? I asked.

The grimace on Smoke's face showed of frustration asking his question the third time.

"I already done asked you twice! What do you want?

Knowing I didn't have authority to speak for the club nor had talked to Paul I spoke the only words that came to mind.

"Mutual respect," I answered, drawing an even more frustrating expression on the president's face.

A moment of silence fell in the room and he responded again.

"And what about our colors?"

"I can't make any decisions for the club, I'll have to have a meeting with my pres. I'll get in touch with him when I leave." Not knowing if my leaving was a certainty but hopeful my answer would influence them.

Trying to add insurance, I said.

"Give me a number and I'll call you as soon as I call and talk to him."

The room remained silent. Knowing I had not accomplished anything I felt it was time to leave. It was made plain that there would be trouble getting our two sets of colors back in trade for theirs. However, remaining at a stand still meant more people could wind up dead.

Smoke gave me a number to call, which gave a sense of security on walking out the door with my life, but I still had to turn my back.

I didn't offer my hand at that point to him or any of the other bikers, not knowing how it would be accepted; instead the door was the next advance.

Moving toward the door, I said,

"I'll get back to you in a few."

The same one that let me in rushed in front of to see me out the door. When it opened I could see light, but still wasn't sure I would make it to my car without a bullet in my back. Until I made it into the car nothing was be certain.

Stepping out in the sun-brightened al fresco looking across the street seeing my T-Bird, the reality of my leaving alive was probable.

* * *

I made contact with Paul after the meeting with the Kicks. The news was surprising that I had met with them but at best we still were at a standstill, and now, without proxy, had stepped in as arbitrator. It was tough explaining the only thing I came away with was they were willing to give us a mutual respect by leaving us alone and the promise that our colors would never surface again. The Sidekicks had a reputation for taking the colors of other clubs and hanging them upside down on the clubhouse wall like other outlaw clubs, which indicated that club was either disrespected or the colors were those of a club where all the members patched over to another club.

Paul wasn't enthused over the idea of surrendering the bargaining tools we put our lives on the line for. It was only firsthand the idea seemed too risky, leaving the uncertainty of embarrassment once again after the bloodshed surrounding four sets of rags. We were both deadlocked but had to make up our minds knowing we had bitten into a wormy apple and the fact was that among the colors we took one of the sets was from another chapter out of another state. Not only had we sent out a perilous invitation in Detroit but nearby Ohio in addition.

Over the next two days I remained in contact with Silver Smoke. He let me know that though they would never like us they had respect for me, and the fact we made an uncalculated move that other clubs in the city would have never done. He also explained that the colors could not be returned because they had been destroyed. We didn't believe it but came to a zenith with the understanding that our colors never show up again in their possession.

My club agreed to return their property trusting they would keep their word. We also let them know that we would not be against more rag swapping if ours resurfaced. Since I was the one who had started the arbitration I personally delivered their colors to them at their house. This time I met a few more of the members, some introducing themselves and some kept a distance. A couple even walked up to me and told me they didn't like us but they now respected us.

The Sidekicks kept their word to that point, us the mutual respect we requested in our part of the agreement. It spite of our differences it showed that guts are sometimes more effective than bullets. Believing words more powerful than that of war my intuitions proved true. Not only did they keep their word as any man of honor would I became friends with those who may have taken my life. Besides, they had to know I was just as much fool as them for walking into a clubhouse with a noose by myself with the number of enemies I had in the house because of the patch I wore on my back. Before long I became a regular at their Friday night parties, not only receiving respect but tokens of love given by bikers. The first token ever given me was by Magic, and was a Combat Infantry Badge but I later had to stop wearing it once an infantry man challenged me wearing it, but it was that kind of love the Sidekicks shared. I met Devil, Porky, Thunder, who they called the Godfather, Bushrod, Mike Dog, Capt. Crunch, the one who turned out to being the one present at our first meeting when my head was on the table, and many more. The list went on but the one I became most close with was like the mascot of the club, Cisco Kidd. Once we got to know each other he'd never cross by path without speaking just all those who had become to accept me. After all, I was still wearing colors some wanted to shoot the monocle right out of that left eye. I met more Sidekicks than I knew of my own members. Their idea of brotherhood was different than what I was used to in the more civilian biker world; they showed me another type of biker love contrary to that I'd received.

After the word traveled throughout the city that the feud had been settled the atmosphere of the biker world changed as well. Those who had been feeling threatened by the Kicks had a renewed confidence in being able to hold a party on their party nights without having them crashed or their motorcycles taken. Not only was I given a visa to go where I wanted and when, I was given a reputation to go with my name.

Now I had the responsibility to uphold it.

CHAPTER 13: RIPPED OFF

The nightlife of the urban biker grew on me like it did all who participated. My need for cash increased, as did my desire to hustle as in all my past. Spending many hours throughout the day practicing my craft in the deejay booth I built, from time to time throughout the day bikers from other clubs stopped in to grab a beer, shoot some pool or play pinball and maybe smoke a joint and chill for a few. There was always someone at the clubhouse because we relied on the revenue of the residents in the neighborhood who came by regularly to shoot pool and spend a dollar here and there. Clearly seen, I was in the ideal location to make some money. While no longer into selling hard drugs, the idea came to mind to sell some weed. It was the only thing I could see myself being involved with after my nearly ten-year ordeal of fighting a heroin addiction. Besides, hustling had been in my blood from childhood.

The neighborhood was a prime location for selling drugs of any kind. It was also the exact location on the east side where the infamous Frank "Nitty" Usher hung out and made his mark in the drug business. Our club was on the very block and next to the store he ran at one time. I showed up only a short time after his incarceration related to the notorious beheadings of two who supposedly had betrayed him. There was very little presence of the police in the area and nobody in the weed game for me to compete with. I just had to figure out how to get a plan in action without the club being tied into my idea and keeping it out of the clubhouse.

Hoping in part I could use my dedication shown to the club would aid me in bringing forth an idea that would allow me the opportunity to sell weed while at the clubhouse. I talked about it to my new president, Mack Man, who had taken Paul's place. He told me I would have to bring it to the body so it could be voted on. Mack Man was the senior in the club and figured he would be the hardest one to get the idea past. Paul was still an active member in the club who had stepped into retirement after losing his incumbency to Mack. I felt that the most opposition would come from those who would be envious or want a piece of the action. What made me take the gamble was the fact there weren't any members in the house who were drug dealers or impressed me as someone who would want to move in on my plan. Paul and Mack Man had jobs and worked everyday during the time I was most present at the club. Less than half of the members in the house smoked weed and the other half didn't really seem to care. I figured the ones who did wouldn't oppose because it would mean smoking for free.

At the next meeting I brought my idea to the table of me selling weed in the clubhouse. Everyone knew of me being key in establishing new revenue generating ideas since becoming a member in the club. My short fame as being the key negotiator in the Sidekick dispute only boosted my chances of getting an approval. When bringing up the idea I felt like the dope dealer of old days, trying to turn the clubhouse into my new dope house. Mack Man didn't smoke any weed though Paul did. I hoped the fact of me always having good personal weed to smoke would give Paul the insurance he could get good product without having to buy it in the streets as well.

When the club voted on my idea I was totally astounded. I got more than asked for. Not only did they agree to let me sell it, but also they made it law that I was the only one who could do it to keep away in-house competition. Glee was an understatement. Knowing that I could spend my wasted time making some money and reestablishing another business gave me a new light and a chance to make more friends and contacts.

Having the club's approval left me the go ahead to find a new clientele. I already knew enough people in and around the club to get rolling. The only thing needed was a source to supply me and be consistent. I had that too. An old friend named Mack, a true-to-the-game old head happened to be an individual I admired notably. He was an entertainer, hustler, 'Mac,' and a *real* player. I'd been acquainted with him since the late sixties after meeting him through Charles who was also in the family through marriage. He always appeared to be in control of what he did and remained conscious of his health and diet. He knew about the streets and about women.

Mack had a connection that sold him pounds of weed. Marijuana had tripled in price over the last ten years and sold for between three and four hundred dollars a pound as opposed to the seventy dollars it sold for in the late sixties. Not having enough money to buy a pound I started off with a quarter and paid a c-note for it.

The return on my investment was great. I tripled my money every time and still gave out nice quantities in order to build my clientele, offering what they couldn't get anywhere else. The booth, sitting in the rear of the shotgun style building became my second home like a bird on a perch, arms and all. I had a .30 cal. M-1 carbine in arm's reach in case someone got ideas though it was highly unlikely because of the stigma associated with motorcycle gangs as being hands off but we knew everyone in the neighborhood. The guns weren't for the people in the neighborhood, but for protection against anything unexpected.

I operated my business just like the legitimate ones on the block and kept business hours. Because we always hung out into the morning hours I'd sleep at the clubhouse on many occasions. Within a short period of time after nine a.m. the doorbell would begin ringing. The more I sat in the deejay booth the better I got at playing music and the more weed I sold. The business district and the usual in and out traffic of the club camouflaged my dealing as well as could be. Within three months I doubled my buys, mostly selling ten-dollar bags throughout the day, I picked up on young and old customers in the hood who became my regulars. A few of the older customers bought ounces to last them a while and keep them from being obvious making trips in the club to see me.

* * *

We hung out late one night. It was 2 a. m and winning color count at one of the clubs where the one with the most members won a half-gallon of liquor. It was a hell of a time to start drinking, but it was no worse than playing tackle football on concrete floors in the clubhouse after we finished most of the bottle.

Returning late one night Elmer J. Ice Man, and me wound up being the ones crashing at the club. Once in and the bar put on the door, nobody could get in without ringing the thunderous door bell that made one awaken when rung once if even drunk. Those who rung it most only touched it.

The bell rang earlier than usual that morning. I knew it wasn't one of my customers. Ice Man got up and opened the door. Pepper, one of my club members had come to see me. He didn't smoke weed but said he wanted to get some for one of the chicken heads he was hanging out with in the hood. I got up and went to my stash to fetch the dime bag of weed. I entered the booth and made it a few steps to where I kept the bag. It was gone. I panicked, while at the same time remembering that Elmer J. was the only one who disappeared over the course of the night and was nowhere to be found. Nobody had come in when we were asleep but the back door was open because it had to be locked from the inside.

Not being able to service my club brother and seeing how pissed off I was, he left, my anger brewing. The weed that was in the bag was all I had except for two hundred dollars left in my pocket. It was only half of what was needed to buy the pound I'd graduated to, leaving me confronted with the possibility of having to ask my click for a consignment deal. I knew that Elmer J. took my weed but since he didn't smoke I figured he had sold it or put it away until he figured the heat would be over.

I waited for him to show up so I could meet face to face with him, knowing he would lie and tell me he didn't take it but he was the only one who had disappeared when the weed did. He showed about four or five hours after the steam realizing my loss and walked in. Confronting him and asking him about it my instinct was to threaten him with my carbine. By time I could grab the gun, he broke out the back door that was his way in and out. His running only intensified my anger and I took off after him, running through the alley and onto the block.

As he ran for his life I raised the gun, running behind. It wasn't my intention to shoot him but couldn't let him get away with his dirty move on me. I took perfect aim at his back, but not wanting to kill him I lowered the rifle and pulled the trigger. Before the sound echoed through the streets his running gait turned to a limp. My rage overwhelmed the idea I was shooting someone wearing the same patch in commonness, a brother. Lowering my weapon, the adrenaline flow ceased and the guilt set in. I thought about the fact the weed was worth less than hundred dollars and if I had killed him I'd be going to jail for the rest of my life for nothing, and though only shooting him in the leg he could have bled to death by the time he made it to the hospital.

By time the police showed up asking questions and for the firearm that was involved in the shooting I had taken it to a hiding place they wouldn't find it if they wanted to search the club for it. The news about what had happened began making its way through the 'hood first by and through the people on the street that saw me as the shooter. As if I had become a hero, people that suspected him of doing wrong to them started showing up as if to congratulate me. I wasn't proud nor did I have my weed back. He was now in the hospital and I wasn't in any better shape. Adding injury to my insult and confirming my intuitions, Popeye, one of the regulars who hung out with the club got a chance to smoke some of the weed Elmer J. stole. He taunted me about how good it was. He knew the person where Elmer J. took it for safe keeping until he could find a buyer and gave that person some to smoke.

Only a few days after Elmer J. ripped me off I hit the number for eighteen hundred dollars. I thought about Nan's words, telling me about getting things taken back tenfold. This was the case, and it left me in a position to buy much more than I could afford in the past. The club didn't kick me out for shooting Elmer J., but banned me from ever becoming president of the club, labeling me a "hothead." He didn't press charges against me, which renewed my license to roll.

CHAPTER 14: GOING LEGIT

Less than a year after starting my new business I was established like an old bank. Not like selling cocaine or heroin, the money was enough for me to do what I wanted including playing thirty dollars a day on the lottery and affording breakfast at Corrine's, the greasy spoon restaurant only a few doors down from the club. Elmer J. recuperated except he walked with a limp for quite a while. I didn't have any more trouble and nothing ever came up missing again.

Not only establishing my business in the neighborhood, it was established too at almost every motorcycle club I went to. I had become known in a short time to be the one most consistent and having the best product around. It got to be to the point that all I had to do was show up and the sales would begin without solicitation. Though the majority of the bikers didn't smoke, there were enough to keep me in a business worth having.

Paul came to me with the idea of re-opening a beer and wine store next to our clubhouse. The idea sounded good in light of my past interest in having a legitimate business. The neighborhood was excellent. There were many households with children and within walking distance. It was an idea that didn't take much thought because we could rent the store from the landlord who also owned the clubhouse.

I took Paul up on the idea of opening the store with a third partner, Big O. The weed was paying nice and was enough to produce my needed share of expenses for the mom and pop style sweet shop. It was a good plan and a way for me to escape the world of hustling as a primary way of surviving. Owning a store was a way to build up more than an entrepreneurship, but a way of having an upstanding name in the community.

We entered into a management agreement with the prior owners of the store and the ones who still had the liquor license. We made a deal with them that would allow us to operate the store including the sale of beer and wine while we waited for approval of our license application that was known to take many months if not years to get approved.

Our biggest expense was security and inventory. The building had a cooler, racks and enough shelving to open the doors once again. We made a commitment and a rule not to touch the money and let it grow to build an inventory and grow to the point we could remodel the store and possibly expand into the building next door.

In a matter a months our inventory had quadrupled. We even hired a few part - time employees. The few racks we had were replaced with new vendor supplied equipment with their names that made the store actually look like a party store. Our cigarette purchase grew from cartons to cases and the cooler was filled to capacity with beer, wine and pop. Big O turned out irresponsible because he was too nice and vulnerable to the young females who feathered his neck, making him forget about the cash register and the seriousness of the business; so we bought him out.

After completing a storehouse of paperwork and proof of incomes from Paul and me, and waiting almost a year, almost giving up on the idea we would be granted a license. I couldn't help but to think the hold up would be due to my criminal past. Nevertheless we continued to grow. The only problem was that the business really wasn't ours because someone else's name was on the main part of it.

With almost a year of waiting, the commission issued our license but not without telling me they knew about my record and told me that if any of my charges had been drug related the license would not have been granted. Unlike most jobs and careers, the licensing commission gave me a chance to make a legitimate living for myself.

In less than an a year after we opened the doors the liquor license was in our name and I was given the chance and opportunity to make a living that I thought would be impossible because of my past criminal record.

Paul and me picked up on the idea of supplying beer and wine to at least half of the fifteen clubs that partied during the week. We added a second cooler in the store, rented a building behind it and turned it into a warehouse that came to house hundreds of cases of beer and wine. Feeling the sense of being a legitimate businessman, the only problem was that I was still selling illegal drugs. I had a business that was clearing me at least five hundred a week without having to go anywhere. I still hadn't reached the affordability of putting myself on the payroll in the store. Nevertheless, it still wasn't time for me to stop. The last year and a half I'd spent building a clientele was just beginning to pay off.

We set our operating hours from 8am to 2am the next morning and hired several employees who consisted of girlfriends, family, and well-known trusted people in the neighborhood. The business continued to grow as well as our inventory. My status as a businessman flourished. Suddenly, I found myself living above any status achieved during the time I was rolling back in the 'hood I grew up in. Forgetting about much of my past, I could focus on a future that brightened by the day. Three years passed since walking away from the dog food and the dog life. The business was making enough revenue that allowed me to be put on the payroll, but it still wasn't as much as I was spending. Motorcycles were my hobby; women were like bees, and I had the honey. Having a motorcycle alone was the only tool needed to pick and choose from the bad girls' mommas never knew they had. Most of them just wanted to ride, but riding alone was my preference. When they knew we were going to take a ride they were like broke shoppers looking through store windows. I had a rule though made known expressed by a sticker on the fuel tank; "Gas, grass, or ass; nobody rides free." It kept many of them from asking, and the few that did ride didn't buy the gas.

The life and money placed me in the better of times I had seen since before I had been shot ten years prior. Not only walking away from an ugly past, I walked away from the name attached to it, no longer using the name "Sonny." I had two businesses next door to each other. In less than two years I had more than ever. It was time to make the move of getting out of the weed business, but that was much of the element that placed me on the second floor. It was a business that I had put two years in and it was just beginning to reap the rewards of my labor. Just walking away from it would be like walking away from any other business someone has worked hard to establish.

It was easy to foresee though that with the expansion of the business our revenue would increase tremendously, allowing me to go totally legit. Our plans included new shelving, lighting, painting, matching Formica counter shelving and counter that had a wide, lighted built in candy case. The entire thirty-foot counter would be cased in bulletproof glass with two turnstiles and two cash registers, and the ability to better handle customers during rushes. I made a vow with myself to let go of the business that afforded me the opportunity to get in the position I was in as soon as we remodeled.

The idea took three months to plan and would have to be executed in less than a week to keep from losing a revenue that was averaging more than five hundred dollars a day, excluding the deliveries to the clubs that we would be able to still service while shut down.

Not being able to afford contractors to do the work for us, I used the skills Nan taught me, along with the basic electrical skills through electronics classes taken a few years after I finished school. Once we were notified that all the shelving and custom carpentry and glass was ready we made our move. Building and remodeling was in my blood. Nan was one of the best carpenters I knew and when she let me remodel her kitchen as a teenager it gave me working experience. On many of the trips we took downtown together created an enthusiasm from watching how department stores like J.L. Hudson operated. I was always enthused at how they could change the whole floor by doing a section at a time and still keep business going and in the end, removing partitions that revealed an updated refashion than was unseen to shoppers on the same floor.

With anticipation of being closed a week at most, our goal was to finish the job in four to five days. Our clientele was dependant on our business being open on time every morning. Many of our deliveries were made before nine a.m. We put notices out that we would be temporarily closed and put hold on the deliveries. On the Sunday night we closed down the dimly lit convenience pantry we had already begun dismantling and packing away merchandise that was behind an old wall that served as the cashiers window whereby customers had to walk forty feet to the back of the store to make a purchase.

We gave everyone who worked in the store a job to do during the alterations, keeping them on payroll and having the woman's touch we needed to make sure everything was presentable and dust free when we reopened the doors. Paul took off a week from work. We kept the three people employed at the store to assist us, keeping them on the payroll during the shutdown period and helping us to cut cost.

What took place over the next three days was short of a miracle. Everything fell into place without incident or slowdown. We painted the walls a sunflower yellow and I suspended the ceiling, adding fluorescent lighting throughout. The carpenter installed the long lime-green counter and matching shelves and bulletproof glass that began at the front of the store, running to the back. The mason did brickwork in the front of the store, adding a few more feet of usable space. We put in additional shelving with aisles and stocked them to the hilt. And in three long days and one night we reopened the doors on Thursday morning at eight a.m.

The place was beautiful. When the light switch toggled the whole building lit up with fluorescent intensity lighting twelve hundred square feet of a subliminal appetizer. We fell short of nothing, including air conditioning behind the enclosed glass partition – keeping the cashiers and the candy cool. The top shelves on one side of the enclosure included a full line of hair supplies to accommodate the then popular Gheri Curl. On the other side we stocked many hard to find items, including feminine products, oils, first-aid, cigarettes, snuff, and goods that couldn't be found for miles. The lighted candy case built into the counter was filled with every type of chocolate bar and confections, positioned eye level to a child and easy to decide on a purchase. We also included a freezer filled with ice and enough groceries that made a trip to the closest market, which was a mile away, sometimes unnecessary.

Tired, from a three-day marathon I sat in my car in front of the store to see the shock on the customer's faces as they walked in. Having been down less than a week some of the regular patrons that last visited on the weekend walked in as were awe struck. They couldn't believe their eyes. Some of them thought we had sold the store to the Chaldeans or Arabs that were making major moves to own most of the neighborhood convenience stores. It was a sign that being a successful entrepreneur was achievable to anyone with the desire.

I knew anything accomplished in life would be, in part, due to Nan's teachings. I remembered her words telling me that one day I would thank her for the butt whippings she gave me when I was younger. Now, my achievement gave me ability to pay her a visit and give her the thanks revealed in her prophecy.

I thanked her with gratefulness.

CHAPTER 15: COCAINE

Heroin was on the downfall in the streets in the early eighties. Almost everyone who visited the West Coast returned with stories of freebasing; smoking soda dried cocaine in glass pipes. I'd heard rumors of the intense high it gave and how it made some people real kinky and craved after smoking it, producing multiple repeat sales until one had spent all their money. It was only a matter of time before it would make it East. *Drugs carry over like clouds and rain.*

For years, cocaine was always classified as the rich-man's drug because only he could afford it.

I wondered.

How in the hell can these motherfuckers get hooked on some shit they can't afford?

I knew of the rush cocaine induced but had never heard of it being smoked, except for putting the powder in a cigarette.

Focusing on my new venture I'd long become disinterested in ideas of organizing a business selling cocaine; besides, I had a liquor license so that type of activity was beyond me. Most of the self-controlled people I used to sell *'boy'* to were making the switch, ascertaining the craft of cooking cocaine powder into rocks and waiting for the curious.

Knowing it had always been quite profitable; I knew money would start to flow in the streets and some into my cash registers, but again, the subconscious hustler Dormant in my subconscious wouldn't let me go without thinking about how much money that could be made. I didn't have the desire to get back in the game like that. I'd never sold enough cocaine in the past to consider making a change that required establishing a new clientele, one with money; but if this thing was as powerful as claimed it could pay off. From the stories, it would also get crazy. With the storm being on the way, I waited for the lightening to let me know when to take cover.

By late 1982, thunder could be heard in the distance. Compared to the first drops of rain were those who diligently waited to get a puff off the pipe that would send them into short-term lunacy were experiencing their first lessons in freebasing. Indications of the storm were obvious as the clouds began covering blue skies of what would turn out to be many.

Upon talking to an old acquaintance of mine named Ben, who I turned my *boy* customers over to back in '79, told me he was making the switch as well. I questioned his ability of handling a dangerous business like that. He was too nice and just wasn't cutout for it, but his adoration for money changed all that.

I decided to pay him a visit.

Upon walking through the door, all I could see was Ben's face sporting a smile that stretched a mile long to the corners of his mouth, from ear to ear. His balding head as well as his mug reflected a brightness of the sun.

"What up?" I asked.

"I ain't never made this much money!"

"Are things that good?" I questioned as he continued to grin.

"I done made eight-hundred since last night!"

Sometimes I didn't make that much money in a week hustling *boy!* I sighed.

We talked about the process of cooking cocaine powder into rocks that would fetch anywhere from twenty-five to a hundred dollars each. He told me how the customers would return to buy more as quickly as they could smoke what they'd just bought.

"You ever tried it?" he asked.

"No."

"You want to try it?"

Seeing that I'd tried everything else mentionable.

"Why not!" I responded.

He turned on the stove and put on a pan of water, sat down and began to measure the *coke.* He added a pinch of baking soda to what he put on a *'coke-board'* and put it all into a small, glass, fire resistant test tube then added a little water.

When the water in the pot boiled, he gyrated the tube around in the hot water several minutes. When the process was finished he added fresh water in the tube and poured the contents onto a nylon stocking over the sink. All that remained was a little white rock. He placed that on a saucer.

I tried smoking a small piece of the pebble that resembled the appearance of rock salt, only whiter, but the euphoria from it wasn't analogous to good cocaine, and it just didn't taste like it.

I passed the next time the plate was.

I couldn't see what people were freaking out about and spending so much money for.

* * *

Months later, through Mack, who also made the switch from selling weed to cocaine. I learned Ben hadn't been selling real cocaine base. The stuff he was getting was mostly speed. It didn't surprise me though, cause like I knew, he wasn't cut for the game anyway; he was the working type family man. What was mysterious was how people inadvertently bought it, *thinking* they were getting the real thing. That demonstrated that people would, and still will, do anything to get high – even if it means using something of unknown contents and origin.

After returning from a tour overseas, Mack also became impacted by the bluster for rock demand. His clientele for those who snorted powder became intrigued with the more intense high. One day I went and talked with him. Although I'd changed games, I've always enjoyed talking to someone with common sense and an understanding of life.

Mack had it.

His shop was set-up in the basement of his rented flat. As we began to talk, he reached under the bar counter and brought up a small white saucer, with the remains of what looked like tiny pieces of base, and sat it on the counter. He reached behind a line of empty Remy-Martin boxes and retrieved a freebase pipe that had been named *Dino,* a glass figurine modeled into a dinosaur.

Reaching under the bar again he picked up a small stainless steel container, half-filled with rum and a pair of hemostats that pinched a swab of cotton.

Gathering a few of the crumbs, he dropped them into the small, screen-laden bowl that extended from the hump in Dino's back. Dipping the cotton into the vessel of rum, he picked Dino up and held the swab for me to light. Putting the tail to his mouth and a finger over the air outlet he began to take a light toke, just enough to melt the base.

He dipped the swab again. I gave him another light. Placing the flame over the bowl, he pulled slowly. About ten inches long, Dino filled with a brilliant cloud of unstained white fog. He held the smoke in a moment then blew it out.

Dino was still filled with haze as we resumed talking.

Placing the pipe to his mouth a few moments later, he pulled the remainder of smoke from the tail, returning the original clarity to the glass once again.

He sat Dino on the bar and pushed the saucer my way.

As if knowing what I was doing, I placed about the same amount in the stem as he did, dipped, and Mack lit the torch.

I attempted to melt the stuff just as he did, re-lit the swab while I exhaled to gain full access to my lungs. I began to drag. At first I pulled too hard. He coached me.

"Pull slow," he directed then paused.

"Pull slow. Let it fill!"

Dino's body swelled with fog.

"Let it fill. Here, let me show you!"

He took the hemostats bearing the blaze and held them over Dino's stem until his belly filled with smoke. He removed the flame.

"Now, pull."

I drew 'til his pout was empty.

After a few seconds I felt a sensational rush that started in my stomach and quickly moved upwards to my head and outwards to every extremity in my body. It was nothing I'd ever experienced. I became light-headed and was hit with a sense of euphoria. Snorting cocaine had never induced a high that powerful.

Goddamn!

The storm had finally arrived.

I pushed the plate back to Mack and sat there in another dimension.

No sooner than he began talking again I started to gaze at the stuff left on the saucer, waiting for him to take another hit and pass it my way again, but he was in no hurry. As usual he was in full governance.

I realized that the nation was going to be in grave trouble when this shit really surfaced. None of the drugs I'd encountered in the past touched that high.

We discussed the urge it produced and the anxiety to attain that first rush.

"It's all about control! She's a hoe, and hoes always lookin' for tricks!. She's supposed to make you money like all hoes! You don't never let her pimp you. You don't be weak for nothin' that's weaker than you!"

Those words of advice were wise, but I already knew I'd never let it get the best of me from what it took to escape the world years behind. Along with Mack's word of the wise I remembered my mother's most poignant words also.

"It's not what you do, it's how you do it!"

Her wisdom was invaluable, but I'm sure not intended for something as insane as smoking cocaine, yet the words remained applicable.

As the high dissipated I bid Mack good-bye and split.

On the way back to my store I gave a lot of thought about what was going to happen when freebasing caught hold – like heroin did in the early to mid-seventies. I figured anyone selling it would get paid, and anyone using it would never be able to keep the money they made; not something I was interested in.

I thought about how *'girl'* had always been the lady's choice. Once they got hold to *this* shit it was going to have them doing anything to get it, including any and every type of sex act imaginable because of the uncontrollable craving it created after smoking it. It could only lower the esteem in women who would allow men to take advantage of them in permissible ways unheard in the past. I knew it was only a matter of time before beautiful women all over the world would offer *all* of themselves for crumbs, literally.

CHAPTER 16: THE GUN I COULDN'T BUY

Months passed. The business continued to flourish. Our daily income had quadrupled from when first opening the doors. On Mondays I had the responsibility of taking the deposit to the bank that included all the money made over the weekend. At a minimum I carried thousands to the bank, most of which covered the checks we wrote at the end of the week that had not yet reached the bank.

We had employees whose lives were slowly becoming dangerous because of the growing cash flow. Though protective glass protected the cashiers from the public, it still wasn't enough to put us at ease. Because Paul and me were known members of a motorcycle club we didn't fear trouble that most did in business because we were bikers and were always feared. Those in the neighborhood knew if they sought trouble they could find it with us because of the war everyone in the 'hood knew about. While Paul and me were the owners of the store, it was seen as a business ran by the motorcycle club. Nevertheless, I now had employees and money to safeguard.

146 Guns, Drugs, Gangs, and Anger

While it was a slim chance we would be prime targets of the stick up man. It wasn't about taking chances. I knew if I ever got robbed making a trip to the bank the loss would put us in bad with our creditors while dozens of checks bounced around until we would be able to cover them with the receipts from the following week. And though the money would eventually be recuperated, making up thousands of dollars would depreciate our inventory, leaving us without our daily purchase of cigarettes and other goods that generated most of our revenue.

While we still had the carbine I shot Elmer J with that remained in the store, it was something that couldn't be carried to the bank. Paul, had no blemish on his record so he applied for and was approved for a concealed weapon permit. We knew because of my past, me being approved was something far-fetched. Nevertheless, I handled the money more and was responsible for keeping my eye on the money. It wasn't about taking chances and putting the business in jeopardy by happenstance.

Having the ability to obtain almost anything I wanted, some of which came from hustlers and cohorts in the neighborhood, Paul found someone with a .38 revolver that was brand new for sale; almost identical to the one ten years ago. Outside of being stainless steel it was an exact replica of the one I had, including the four inch barrel.

Not only concerned about keeping everyone safe, including my newfound fiancé who now worked in the store, I felt it was time to seek ownership of a legal weapon to protect everything. Quite aware of my prior criminal record, even with doubt, I had to at least see if I could get some special permission that would allow me to be able to carry a gun to the bank and back to the business. My only hope was the fact that my state liquor license would make things easier, possibly enabling me to own a legal firearm at least in my place of business.

I also learned that the only way of owning a gun was through a forgiveness of the felonious crimes I had committed years before. Learning the feds were the ones that could grant me a letter of pardon or exclusion, I went to the department of Alcohol, Tobacco and Firearms with my request.

I took the ten-mile trip downtown to the Federal Building and went to see the same folks I lived my life avoiding. My request would be to get permission to carry a firearm during my trips to the bank, to and from the business. Figuring all along they would never give me the privilege to carry a gun as I would liked to have had, my hopes was that I could at least have a gun in my place of business.

Entering the office of the feds the vibrations didn't give me the feeling I was in company of those who cared why I was there. One of the agents enquired as to what they could do for me. I explained my situation to one of the officers in the room who then went to the other agent and told my story. Learning about my past after running my name through their system, the officer returned to where I sat with a smile on his face and a look of contentment. Sitting less than ten minutes waiting to hear to decision of the adjudicators the one who waited on me returned.

When the cop-cut agent returned to give me an answer to my request he walked over to me with a smirk on his face ready to render his remarks.

"Mr. Woods, you said you wanted a gun to protect you business and your assets, is that correct?

"Yes. I'd like to have protection in my place of business to protect our assets as well as the employees that worked for us," I responded.

The look on his face was obviously leading to humiliation seeing he had found the fool of the day.

"Let me explain something to you. If someone comes in your store and robs you and you shoot them, we're going to put YOU in jail," the Fed told me.

It then set in that regardless to what license I might have had, I was still a felon and owing a gun was the last thing I would be allowed to have. While law may have dictated their reasons, I had to make the decision to protect the assets of the business and make my own rules irrespectively. The choice the Feds left me was that I had to make choices of my own. Getting caught again carrying a second time could not only jeopardize my name on the business but as well put me in jail because I would be a three time felon and guaranteed jail time.

Getting caught a second time without a gun could also lead to the loss of my life. Surviving another a stickup with an armed gunman was pushing the odds. The mental agony of surviving another near fatal trauma made my mind up for me. I wasn't about to get caught with major money that didn't belong to me; it belonged to the business. I was in a Catch 22. Either I be caught carrying a gun or be caught without one. The latter decision was one I couldn't afford.

* * *

Another year passed. The business continued to do well. Most of the time the cash register rang without end. I dropped the weed business and decided to go for it without the money that that supported much of my pastime. I got married and had begun making my move toward settling down and starting a family. While the money I made in the store wasn't quite enough, it was enough to keep gas in my bike and my car, allowing a few dollars on the lottery. My luck had been paying off and the lottery helped put a few bucks in my pocket.

Still hanging out into the early morning hours at the biker clubs while trying to run the business began taking a toll on my body and mind. Though we had employees that opened the store and ran it most of the time, when they didn't show I had to take their place. Because of our hours of operation, I still had to be available most of the eighteen hours we were open. If

I weren't needed to go to the wholesale everyday, there would be something that would take any free time. Even on my day off, most times I got called to sign more checks for our distributors or make a trip to buy cigarettes at the least. When trying to buy enough merchandise to eliminate a trip to the wholesale the next day, there would always be something to send me back.

The shelves were stocked to the hilt; self-sufficiency seemed to be at hand, yet I began tiring of the daily routine. Unlike most storeowners that usually grew up in a family business and had it in their genes to work hard all day, I was a hustler from the streets, not someone to be tied down to a post or anything. Growing up doing what I wanted most of my life, the importance of freedom began outweighing the value of having a business.

Our investment had by far reaped a hundred fold. As most partners, Paul and me had a few disputes sparingly which weren't about much of anything. Most of the time I would antagonize him about how he treated the ladies we had working for us. He expressed an authoritarian manner of cracking a whip and like many job supervisors it was a natural routine. It was plain to see that he was one who had lived taking orders, giving the same to all under his leadership. Having been an incumbent president through a number of elections, he was used to giving orders accompanied with a hint of arrogance. I was one who didn't take orders and thought that finesse was always the best way to get what you wanted out of people. I remained quite adamant about practicing it and reminded him that dogging people in the club was something he could get away with, but harassing the people who handled our money was like biting the hands that fed us.

CHAPTER 17: SHORT OF HOMICIDE

While it had only been four years since opening the doors of the store, the need to take some time off seemed more important than the daily routine. I hadn't taken a vacation since we opened the doors. A dispute with Paul and my quick temper led me to make the decision to take off some time that I would normally not have taken off had it not been for our disputes.

During my time off the squabble grew and upon continuing to pay myself, Paul chose to lock me out of the business. Because we had legal agreements drawn when we first opened the business, I knew he didn't have anything coming, leading me to think that the documents would protect my assets so I sought legal counsel while I played along. There was no way I could go back to work once the courts were involved and figured his move would put the ball in my court. At the worst we would have to put the business up for sale or reach a mutual agreement.

Not knowing what the outcome of the situation would be I worked in a store owned by one of the gents I'd met since joining the Black Grocers Association. After revealing my problem that I had going on in my dispute with my partner he gave me a job watching his liquor store that was about a mile from mine.

While it felt strange working in someone else's business, not being able to go in my own, it allowed me to make a paycheck to pay the bills at home. Having dropped my weed business the year prior, I no longer had a hustle to supplement my income. As opposed to being the boss, I was someone's employee – something that left me short of self-humiliation. What added a little comfort was that I ran the store when the owner wasn't there and didn't do much of anything. I didn't handle any money, just kept an eye on everything. I was like a security guard without a uniform, just a blue smock like the one the owner wore.

Waiting for my day in court, I showed up for work one day at Mr. Deans Party Store to report for work. When I walked in and went to grab my store jacket he stopped me.

"I'm gonna have to let you go!" he told me.

What!

I couldn't tell whether he was serious or not. He almost always kept a smile on his face, even when he put his cashiers in check. I couldn't think of any reason why he would be firing me. I hadn't stole anything and while he had one of his daughters and another young lady working in the store and the cameras he had in the store wouldn't have given him reason to believe I was trying to get sociable. Besides, I was married and wasn't interested in either one of them.

"Are you serious?" I asked with a bit of hope he was only kidding.

"I can't trust you," he said, still with the grimace of a smile.

I didn't know what to say next. I wondered if he had talked to Paul or picked up some doubt as to my reason for not being in my own store. I didn't bother to question why he thought I couldn't be trusted. It was an insult to my character and a slap in the face. I smiled nevertheless.

"Well, I guess it is what it is!" I replied, knowing my pride was hurt more than I was about losing the job.

My next move was walking toward the door; leaving him standing with the same disingenuous smile he had when he told me. Finding myself like a child without a friend I headed home.

Losing the job was a surprise. Nevertheless, the income had to be replaced without haste. The problem was that asking someone for a job and telling them I was the owner of a functional business would have left clouds over my integrity or leaving them thinking of me as a great liar. It would be a waste of time applying for minimum wage jobs or one that wouldn't be obtainable because of my felony record. Not having other friends with a business or the ability of giving me a job, the only thing that came to mind was to see if my friend Mack might give me some kind of work enabling me to make a few dollars.

I went by to see Mack and told him of my situation. Knowing he didn't have a retail business, the only job he could have for me would be running a few packages or answering the door for him while he attended to other waiting customers. He agreed to do what he could to help me out while I waited to settle my dispute at the store. And since most of his business was done on weekends, my days to work would be few. The major problem I had with the idea of it was the exposure to the drugs on a regular basis. Yet with all the advice Mack had given me about not becoming addicted to cocaine base, there would always be the struggle of keeping from going too far and placing getting high in front of everything else.

As time went on waiting to settle the dispute with Paul in the store my patience grew short. The attorney I hired gave me the vibration he didn't know as much as he claimed. It was time to look at the reality of things if he screwed up. It didn't make sense for him not to do anything that led him to call. I got a good chance to look at what I was actually losing, which was basically half of the wholesale value of the goods in the store. One thing that had always played on my mind was that our true growth was stunted because we didn't own the building and the landlord didn't want to sell. He owned many of the properties in the neighborhood and most of the buildings on our block including the motorcycle club next door to the store and as long as he could collect rent he wasn't selling.

Fact of the matter was that I still had an investment and half ownership of the business Paul and I owned. And I just wanted Paul to give me a fair shake of what we had. I was tired of it after four short years. I still had the psyche of a blessed child who always had his way in life. All that could be seen was hard work, something I was never used to. Being on call and working from morning to morning took a toll on my instability. I didn't see it as everything, but more than I was willing to let him walk away with. I still had a sense of pride and a reputation to protect.

It took almost three months waiting for the court date since me and Paul had the falling out. When I made it to the courthouse I met with my attorney. After speaking with him as to what could be done, he still didn't seem to have any answers about what his course of action would be. I could see he wasn't prepared and only a waste of the seven hundred dollars I gave him as a retainer.

When Paul and his lawyer showed up it didn't much for me to see that he brought a shark with him and I had a goldfish. His lawyer obviously knew his way around the courtroom and did so with arrogance. Paul seemed to be having his way in the courtroom like he had his in the club.

When Paul, me, and the two attorneys who could have been fish stood before the judge, Paul's whale swallowed my guppy lawyer like the worthless feeder he turned out to be. My counsel didn't say much of anything that made sense as the judge heard our case. It was in the legal agreement that in case of a dispute an arbitrator would be used as a third party source of resolution. The problem was that the attorney who drew up the partnership agreement forgot to put in the document that described how things would be distributed in case of entitlement. Paul's counselor accused me of abandoning the business and made it clear that was his strategy to be used in his argument.

Almost ready to grab my lawyer by the throat for standing there like a scared kid, firing him on the spot. My frustration turned to disappointment and anger that began to brew. Not knowing what to say now in front of the judge gave the other team all the steam it needed to pick up speed. All I could do was increase my chances of the obvious loss I was about to experience. The adjudicator adjourned the case allowing me the chance to hire new counsel. I left the courthouse thinking about my predicament.. I didn't have a job, no more money left in the bank, and no income from the store. Hiring another lawyer was something that appeared an improbability. The counsel I had was the most affordable found when hiring him. With Paul having a job that I didn't have and a cash register that could make him a loan at any time left me the vision of losing whatever share I had left.

Almost in a mental state of fury, the reputation, anger, and possibly an irrational mind from my cocaine use left me to take things in my own hands. If I couldn't make any money from the store, neither could he.

It was time to shut it down.

The idea of closing the store was one that wouldn't be easy but the only one that could let him see I wasn't to be screwed over. Paul wasn't the kind of person that showed anything other than he wanted it all, without putting fairness in his intentions. Knowing I couldn't hold anyone hostage or imprisoned, I knew I could keep anyone from going in. The entrance of the front of the building was fitted with wrought iron and an entrance gate canvassing a foyer that led to the access door of the store. With all the things I'd done in my life, taking the chance was something I didn't have to think about twice. So I went and bought a lock, just like the one we had on the store. I wanted Paul to see I had a lock just like his and what it felt like to be on the wrong side of one, like me.

Knowing all the while Paul was strapped it wasn't about to make me change my mind; he couldn't shoot me for locking the door on a business my name was on. Taking precautions, I made sure to carry my piece with me to keep the odds even. I never figured guns would ever be drawn, but if it came to it, I wouldn't hesitate to use it. It wasn't the first time for gunplay.

When arriving at the store I immediately walked up and locked the front gate. Upon looking inside I could see he had a couple of people he was talking to inside. One of them was the landlord, who knew about the dispute, and his brother. It was too late though; I had already made my move. Once the landlord saw what was happening he immediately bided Paul goodbye and headed towards the door where I was, leaving the brother the only one left outside of Paul and his girlfriend who worked as a cashier.

The landlord smiled as he walked up to the door. We spoke. I unlocked the gate and let him out, leaving Paul talking with his brother. Things suddenly weren't going as planned. I didn't expect Paul to be there, especially with so much company. He probably was talking to them about his day in court only hours prior.

It was obvious to see that once I had locked the gate after the landlord was out that Paul and his brother began talking about a way to diffuse the situation. It was two against one but I had my .38 as my backup in case they tried to bum-rush me. I knew I couldn't keep anyone in the place against his or her will, which could lead to me being prosecuted for false imprisonment and making things worse than they already were.

When Paul and his brother walked in my direction I knew I'd have to open the gate to let them out. In case they decided to rush me they would have me outnumbered, yet it wasn't the time to draw a gun.

I opened the lock when Paul said he wanted out. Having an inward swing, when I opened the gate it placed me between the gate and the wall of the entrance foyer. As I attempted to move from behind the gate, he hurriedly pressed his weight against the gate, pinning me. His brother followed with both feet on the gate and his back against the other sidewall, doubling his force. Not being able to move, and my face pressed tightly to a three-quarter inch round piece of steel that supported the security gate.

It became time to defend myself. The pressure of all the weight barely let me budge. Now, with my face against the wall and the two of them behind me, Paul's brother began kicking me through the gate. Struggling to reach for my gun the kicking increased. Fighting the force of all the weight I pushed my hand passed my stomach, leaving skin on the wall in front of me as it scraped over the abrasive wood fascia toward the butt of the gun that was under my jacket.

The kicks through the gate increased, now to the side of my face, forcing the piece of iron to impale my face. Tasting the ore in my saliva I began pulling the trigger to shoot behind, know if I could hit one the other wouldn't be a problem. Paul saw me reaching for the gun but I was about to pull the trigger. The hammer drew back and when it released, Paul had his thumb between the hammer and the firing pin, using his prior military training to save his and his brother's life.

At least for a moment.

The police came after they were called, less than ten minutes later. The pain I was in was overshadowed my humility and defeat. Though my body was wracked with soreness the only thing I could think about was committing a double homicide. I didn't know Paul's brother or where he came from but he became a sudden enemy. Regardless of his brother, he crossed the line into my business and was now responsible for the hole in my face.

The police diffused the situation, learning that I was carrying a gun and also the co-owner of the business. They talked with Paul for a few minutes and took me away, un-handcuffed, to the precinct close-by. On the way I explained my side of the story and left them with the notion to let their superiors handle the situation with the gun and me.

When we arrived at the station the officers took me to the commander of the precinct. Luckily, I was no stranger to him because we had met four years priors when we needed his signature as required in the application of our SDM liquor license. Walking in the door to his office I was assisted by one of the officers who brought me there and handed the, now unloaded, gun to the commanding officer, explained the situation and the information he had gathered. Then he left the room.

I gave details to the White, middle aged, tall slender man who sat behind a gold badge that gleamed authority, the kind I needed to squash a third felony, and the second one carrying a gun. As I talked the officer seemed more focused on the obvious damage to my face that I had not yet seen. When I applied the slightest of pressure to the inside flesh of my jaw my tongue fit through the hole like a key.

The officer who had left out came back with a make sheet on me, along with the history of the gun I had, which was clean and not traced to being stolen.

"You know I can't give you your gun back."

Shit! If I can walk out of here you can have that motherfuckin' gun!

"That's not a problem; I understand, sir," came the response with a sigh of relief and a smile he couldn't see.

"You need to get to a doctor! Your face is really bad," he said.

Looking down at the raw skin on my knuckles, I thought more about revenge than a doctor.

The commander rose from his desk and walked outside of the office, returning only a moment later with an officer who he instructed to take me to the hospital to get stitches that were obviously needed.

I thanked the commander with sincere gratitude and left with the officer, riding in the front seat of the squad car. On the way all I could think about was evening the score. Periodically pushing my tongue through the hole in my face, all I could think about was *Cephus; that's the motherfucker I want!*

Several hours passed before I could get from the hospital and back to my car, which was still parked at the store. When I arrived, the store was closed. Paul knew I would return to get it and perhaps catch him at a time when he didn't have an upper hand. He knew I would be hot as cayenne pepper. The whole block hadn't been that quiet since Christmas.

With three stitches in my face and a bad attitude I got in my car and drove home to my wife, who I had already talked to on the phone when at the hospital. On the drive I was filled with fury. In all my life I had never been on the losing side of battle. This was a war I was ready to start and finish without being a casualty a second time.

By early the next morning the Novocaine injected into my cheek had worn off, leaving me with the reality I had a whole in my face and probably a loss of a small fortune, something that could be regained again. I was a hustler and whatever it took to survive I would make it afloat once again. Having and losing was a way of life experienced by most people in the ghetto where I came from.

Feeling like dynamiting the store, I came to reason with myself. I realized that if I did blow up the store, shoot Paul or his brother, I would be the first one questioned. Not being a good liar in order to get even I'd have to wait until things blew over, requiring me to carry a grudge for months, perhaps years.

Somebody can always rob his ass though and shoot him in the process!

During the wait period I had the chance to think about taking the lives of those who had wronged me. The reputation I stood on diminished, as did the days pass. My family became my focus. I had two children that needed a father in their lives instead of one in jail. The best part of the outcome turned out to be that I didn't leave Paul's kids without a father. Even though I probably would have gotten away with self-defense if I had shot them, I would still have to deal with death on my hands until my dying day – a death sentence in its own. What I lost was material, much less than the value of life. It wasn't necessary to get revenge because God takes care of that for us. If something is done wrong He makes it right. I knew that.

A year later the store closed.

CHAPTER 18: THE LAST GUN

After battling multiple melanomas, a form of cancer, Nan passed in September of 1990. She took with her a part of me never to be relived. Before she died I prayed that she wouldn't suffer and the prayers were answered. The kind of person she was she didn't deserve to suffer and she didn't. I had worked a few jobs the past years after overcoming a battle with pride. I delivered pizzas until getting a job at the Joe Louis Hockey Arena. After becoming single again I got a job driving a cab and enrolled in community college.

Driving the cab was right up my alley. It was a hustle, and I could drive around the city while making money. Already knowing the main streets in the city all I had to do was become more familiar with the street numbers and the streets that had dead ends. Getting caught up on a dead-end street could mean getting beat-out by another cab because in many cases when someone called a cab they called two, taking the first one that showed up. Once learning the streets and the shortcuts it became fun; and even more so around Christmas and New Years.

I leased a cab on a daily basis from the Blue Eagle cab company on West Chicago, about six miles from where I lived in a house that Nan bought in the mid eighties. I drove a few different cabs at first on a half-day lease until later keeping it on a day-to-day basis. Once I took a cab around the clock, getting the chance to pick one of the best taxis he had; the number was 455.

Driving the city and dealing with passengers that would call for cabs to go three blocks away was the worst part of the job. Sometimes I would drive three miles to make the two-dollar fare. And most of the time they wouldn't leave a tip. The best runs were to the airport. Though we didn't get a lot of them in my neck of the woods, when I got one it would pay half the lease for the day.

As twilight approached the clientele changed in comparison. As opposed to making runs taking women to the laundry mat and the nearby shopping centers, the runs mostly went to taking passengers to the nearby dope-house.

I thought about being robbed and shot to death trying to make a few dollars driving a four-wheel hoe. I had one pistol left in my original two-gun arsenal, a .25 caliber automatic. It was just the perfect size to carry without being noticed and would fit in almost any pocket. While it didn't have deadly power, a few to the right place would do the job. Growing up clinging to the cliché I was no different. It was "better to be caught with it than without it."

I was picking up my last fare about three one Saturday morning; I had worked all day Friday and was tired and ready for bed. I had more than made my quota for the day and had made enough that would allow me to sleep late in the morning. A young man entered the cab with a little boy. It was late for a child to be up, but nothing seemed in frenzy. We drove to the corner. No sooner than making a left turn, the police in an unmarked car rode down on us like we had just committed a crime. I first thought they figured I was picking up a passenger moving dope, because that's mostly what's out at that time of the morning.

With the bright spotlight shining from the car and the flashlights pointing into the cabin of the vehicle the light shined into the backseat of the cab. As they began shining the light in the front where I was, separated from the passenger by a bulletproof partition, I hoped they wouldn't see the pistol I'd just slid under the seat when they vamped us. Shining the light in my face, the officer saw the guilt on my mug.

"You want to step out of the car, sir?"

Why the hell aren't they asking that dude in the back to step out? He should be the one under suspicion!

"Are you carrying any weapons or drugs?" The officer standing closest to me, asked his partner to begin searching the front of the cab while the passenger and his son remained in the back seat.

"No, I don't have anything like that!" I protested, knowing his partner's hand was nearing the place where I hid the gun.

Ain't this a bitch! Damn.

No sooner than I thought it, the officer found it. Doing the usual routine, they unloaded it and put the cuffs on me. They told the passenger to walk back home and call another cab; this one was going to the police station. I rode in the back of the police car with the first cop while the other one drove my cab.

Once more, I was handcuffed and put in the back of a police car for allegedly having a gun. Again, for the fourth time I made the same trip to the police station, one time with my hands unbound. The routine repeated itself. I was questioned, locked back up, and questioned again.

While my answers remained unchanged, the two detectives interrogated me like I had been pulling stick-ups or something while I was driving a cab. Every time they asked me about where the gun came from I replied with the same answer.

"I told you I don't know anything about it. It's not mine! I lease this cab. Far as I know whoever drove it when I was off must have left it!"

When they tired of throwing rocks against a wall, I was locked up one last time for the night, and until I went to court the next morning to be arraigned.

Discharged on a personal bond, not having to put any money up for my release, I left the courthouse with the same cash in my pocket I got locked up with. I made the decision to have a court appointed lawyer because those who were paid in the past didn't seem to make the outcomes in my favor.

I caught the bus until close enough to cab it the rest of the way home where my car was parked. Mr. Rucker, the owner of the cab, had someone pick it up from the police station. He didn't bitch about the inconvenience; he just charged me fifty dollars.

I didn't waste time getting back to the station to get my money maker back, before someone else got hold to it. Within a couple of hours of being released I was back on the road. The police had taken my weapon of self-defense, leaving me as prey to the vultures of the night. Still, with a need for support, I drove unremittingly.

* * *

I continued to go to school while waiting for my case to make it to trial. Because the cab was leased and others drove it, I hoped my side of the story would win over in court. Yet, at the preliminary hearing it was established the prosecution had enough evidence to bind me over for trial. The judge handling my case had a reputation for being fair on the bench but I still couldn't trust him because my life was at stake. My young, White, female counselor had never won a case in court; I was her first. The prosecutor, much more experienced could get another feather in his cap by sending me away for a few years, so he pursued.

Waiting for trial I took a good look at the young man in the mirror, seeing someone whose luck had to run out one day. Guns were at the root of most of my problems from day one. I saw someone who would shoot another just for not believing I wouldn't. My anger was obviously uncontrollable. The reflection let me see that I was my own worst enemy and If I didn't eliminate guns from my life they would be my downfall.

In spite of watching my father die from a gun, in my first eighteen years I had already earned the title of "felon" from carrying a gun. In a short two years later I had shot myself and been shot by someone else, almost losing my life. By thirty I had also shot someone else and came within a hair of shooting at least three others. And in the midst of a gang-style was I survived an ambush where everyone in the open got shot with high-powered rifles instead of me.

Like a smart gambler, it was time to call it quits while ahead. I had done everything but time in prison. Withstanding, I now lived on the other side of the fence with those who locked out from second chances and being accepted again once we learn from our mistakes. The only thing now was to accept it and try to fit in with those on the side of the fence where I didn't want to be. Regardless of the kind of person I was at heart, I was one that couldn't be trusted in the eyes of most. The rules were already made before I got here. It was my own ignorance that put me where I wound up.

Unlike those living on the other side of the barrier that made it unscathed, my life was deemed worthless, by law. Though I had a family and a home, I didn't have the right to protect them if it involved me saving us with the use of a firearm. And if all hell broke out and everyone started shooting, I didn't have the right to put on a bulletproof vest to save my life. It wasn't the kind of family I came from; and I felt separated and on the other side of the fence from those I admired most.

While it was a gun that got it all started, it was anger that caused me to harm or attempt to harm someone else. I realized that it wasn't for me to have a gun anyway because I was too quick to use it. Eventually, I would kill someone or someone would kill me, perhaps reaching for it. After the thought of realizing I was the enemy, I became untrusting of the spirit that lived inside and literally scared of myself.

I thought about the conversation Nan had with me about my grandmother telling her that my dad would die with his shoes on. I thought about me doing the same, which was something I hadn't planned on doing, . I envisioned my dad dying in a puddle of his own blood caused by a bullet. The only way possible to keep from following in his footstep was to get rid of the gun in my environment until I trusted myself to be around one.

* * *

Before my trial date I received an unexpected call from my youthful attorney, who fresh out of law school, advised me that in order for the prosecutor to win his case, he would have to prove that I knew about the gun. The main obstacle was the judge because we chose to have a bench trial, where he would be both judge and jury. It was a chance I had to take, better than copping a plea deal that would be sure to add a third felony to my list and probably jail time.

My attorney told me that she had actually researched my case and found a similar one that she could refer to when we went to trial. While there could be doubt about the fact it couldn't be proven I knew about the gun, or the possibility someone else may have left it in the vehicle. It was also still a possibility that the judge could find me guilty if he wanted to. My last chance at freedom lay in the hands of people who didn't know me and weren't expected to care about the outcome.

On the day of my trial I met my attorney outside of the courthouse. She was smiling and bubbly, appearing to smell victory. From all the cases seen where attorneys are appointed by the court, many times I saw people incarcerated who got nothing more from the attorney than a promise to appeal their sentences.

When my turn came for my case to be heard I only thought about the reality of being sent to jail for at least a couple of years because of fitting the profile of a habitual criminal. Though it had been fifteen years prior and I hadn't been in any trouble, the felony charges remaining on my record were still incriminating. Standing before the judge, my faith became my only way out. My attorney made her case to the judge, using the strategy she claimed would be our defense. While the judge sat on the bench the expression on his face were that of someone who had already made up their mind, and hearing the case was all procedure. I began thinking about how much I would be away from my kids and my freedom. Though free on bond, if I was found guilty there was great chance my personal bond could be revoked and I would be sent to jail.

After the prosecution presented its case and my attorney responded to the charges, the judged sat forward in his chair. After only a few minutes me case was heard. His honor sat quiet for a minute, writing notes on the paper work in the case file. My legs weakened before he opened his mouth.

"Sir I find you not guilty."

Turning to my attorney, she smiled, and I returned the same, followed with my thanks and a bear hug. I was free to go; free to make the decision not to be caught up again. All I had to do was stay away from the things that burdened my life. It was a choice already made before walking into the courtroom that day. I took the elevator down to the street floor and walked out of the courthouse and into a life of freedom; one that I now treasured more than ever. I made a promise to myself not to die with a gun in my hand, but as an old man from natural causes with his shoes still under the bed.

CHAPTER 19: LOOKING BACK

Looking back some forty years, for reasons I've always held on to the idea that when I caught that first gun case had I been a young white boy in the suburbs in the early seventies the courts probably never would have known of my existence. Not knowing what the charges meant, the police did. The act of committing a felony was something they knew would be another method of modern age slavery.

Eighteen years of age at the time, it never occurred to me my life literally ended when strapping on a gun that night. Those with felony convictions are nevertheless categorized with hardened criminals whether they go to jail or not. It didn't make any difference being raised in the church and that I was still attending school or that I'd never been in trouble before. Once a felon all those things don't matter. And the job you may have wanted like Mr. Friendly who visited your school as a child is no longer within reach or a possibility.

Nearing sixty years of age I've long been an upstanding figure in my community for many years. My participation in block clubs has always been present, including mentoring young men and taking part in non-violence coalitions. I've almost never missed casting a ballot in an election and have a number children and grandchildren who look up to me. I've made many changes in my life and find myself more honest and trustworthy than most who cross my path. And though having long ago adjusted to the fact I will always be labeled a felon and forbidden from owning a gun or having so much as a bullet to protect my family or myself while living in a crime ridden neighborhood. According to the law, if I have a wife or a female companion that is a gun owner, she must keep the gun under lock and key and away from me. And as unrealistic as that may sound, that doesn't bother me as much as the fact that if all those who had guns began an all out war I would go to jail if I put on a bulletproof vest to protect my life.

While never claiming the stigma attached to the criminal I've been forced to live on top of a fence that divides the good from the bad, not connecting totally with the people on either side. Classified now a senior by many; seniority isn't enough to restore my full rights as an American citizen or make people see me equal to them. The only advantage seems to be is that felons are exempt from jury duty and not forced to put someone else in the same chains.

As one to admit, it all starts with being in the wrong places doing the wrong things at a time in life when the focus should have been on a future and a career. It is plain to see now that if a man's firm hand had steered me in the right direction I'd more than likely be far better off. I thought the hundreds of dollars my penny ante drug dealing was making me weekly would have somehow led me to a stash of millions that I could live off the rest of my life. After realizing that dream would never come true, the battle scars and gunshot wounds wound up being my only compensation. The fast money was a lure, never learning in school or at home the ramifications of being caught with drugs and guns or even having the understanding of what a criminal case was. It's something most have to learn on their own, sometimes from ignorance, sometimes from stupidity and sometimes from just inattention.

What I didn't give a thought to is that once my pockets fattened and the gold and diamonds glittered, someone would be waiting to set me up to take what I had; one thing hasn't changed over the years but gotten worse. Being that luck was on my side, the doctors whose hands were driven by God saved my life. Most aren't that fortunate, which is why so many of us don't make it to old age.

Federal laws make it a point to keep the felon with his/her hands tied. The government knows that most mistakes in life made by the young black male are ammunition to eliminate him from obtaining a successful life by age of maturity. By the time the individual wakes up, in many cases, it's too late. What's worse today than forty years ago is that federal laws attack the young person's education by making laws to exclude those who have any type of drug conviction after 1996, putting them into a lifetime of ostracism. These laws are grenades for the elimination of impoverished people, per say, the black race. Young people from prominent neighborhoods who've made education a priority don't sell drugs on the streets though they may buy them in ghettos from the less fortunate, confirming my reasoning that laws which eliminate one's education is a permanent form of enslavement. Once the conviction is in place, the chances that a person will ever be able to gain a position of employment that will pay for education are nil.

I take full responsibility and ownership of the senseless things I did as a young person. While the first gun case happened in my young ignorance, planning and conspiring to commit insurance fraud with a stolen car years later left no excuse. I knew what I was doing and had plenty of time to think about it, but the idea of a free flashy ride took precedence over the reality of getting caught with it. My stupidity of taking it across international borders was deserving of punishment and meant to teach me a lesson. Nevertheless, that second felony was the nail in the coffin, insurance that the once in a lifetime chance it would be expunged from my record would not be included in my future. The title of felon was permanent. Because many jobs and types of careers excluded me from participation, like most, I had to use whatever skills I knew to make money. In my case, the skills learned in trade school enabled me to add to life's ability to hustle and never go hungry, being able to maintain an honest living. One thing seated in my conscious mind though was that I didn't belong on the other side of the fence with murderers and stick-up artists; but like a puzzle, it was the only place I would be accepted, like it or not.

* * *

Prior to 1968, living in Detroit, and a young teenager; the first moments of real excitement came from witnessing the riot in my hometown and all the civil rights movements going on in the south and elsewhere led by the late Dr. Martin Luther King Jr. The members of the Black Panther Party expressed their contempt from rooftops of buildings in impoverished African American communities around the globe, and Malcolm X was speaking publicly his poignant words against the evil white powers. Though I was really too young to join any type of struggle, I had enough sense to think *these people got to be crazy!* Thinking to what I'd seen on TV how we black folk were being hung in the South and locked up and shot in the North, I knew all these people were setting themselves up to be killed.

It happened.

By late 1969, all black leaders were dead or too scared for their lives to pursue a life of fighting for civil rights; it became too dangerous. A new drug was fed to the community, to further calm the anxiety of those who saw that racism was tiring among people who wanted to be treated fair like most white people, heroin.

What we didn't see then is that we were targets in a plan to stop the protestors, rioters, and revolutionaries. The mission was to divide, conquer, and destroy that dark part of the American world that wanted to be treated fairly, along with their children and their children's children. With the track record of governmental control in many countries it has always been a practice to use opiate and addictive drugs at times to control its people. Knowing the arrogance of the powers that were in control at the time, consciousness confirms my intuition that the government allowed the mafias to distribute the heroin, knowing it would destroy the revolt of the black man along with bystanders young and old who were of no concern, like me. Heroin was the perfect drug for the job; conquering the troublemakers and rioters with an addiction that makes them forget about their families, and jail those responsible for selling it.

It worked. By the mid seventies the structure of family was falling apart. There were drug houses in the numbers on every block in every neighborhood. The plan was working. The police were putting those in jail who didn't have enough drug money to buy freedom and the lawyers were beginning to make more money than ever in defending the offenders, making off with any money they managed to accumulate. It was the first time in my life I began seeing black killing black folk, setting them up to take their cash proceeds. The dealers became feed for many who were out to take what they had, including the lawyers and the judges. Many who were labeled as upstanding in the community also lost their prominence in the raging domination of unconscious warfare with us being pawns, whether from using or selling drugs.

Forty years later,
Of the many people who lost their lives or put them on the line for the quick dollar, if still living, no longer have a penny of the money they made. Many of them died with the dreams that

never became reality. One thing in common among many was the admission that after they got out of drug dealing and before they died was the regret of selling harmful drugs to their brothers and sisters further adding to their demise.

I share in the guilt.

The punishment for my participation is now seeing my young brothers living out the same dreams as their fathers and grandfathers. The difference today is that so many are selling themselves to the system for pennies, never making enough money to pay for a lawyer before ruining themselves for a lifetime. We went through a solid ten years of heroin beginning in the late sixties, five years of cocaine in the early eighties, twenty years of crack, now weed, Ecstasy, and heroin again.

While many born into this world today believe there is a future in selling drugs, the proof of failure is etched in stone and proven by many including myself. What the stick up man doesn't get, the lawyers, courts, and envious friends will. If you are lucky as me (and most aren't) you will escape with your life. As long as we continue to believe there is a future in selling illegal drugs there will be a presence of guns, which are summons for death. It all deals with the law of attraction; where there are guns the chances of someone being shot are far greater than if there were none present. Where there are drugs there are guns to protect them. Where there are drugs, there is someone with their eye on them, just as with and even more than money.

What we must see is that with the onset of drugs not only did we lose our fathers in the home, but our system of values. With no teaching in the family as it was in the sixties and prior, the value of honesty and integrity as men also went out the window with Dad. Now truthfulness, and belief in one's self has no importance among those who have not taken a look in the mirror. A parent into guns, drugs, thievery and wrongdoing can produce children of the same character. And as long as we continue to teach our kids drug dealing we'll continue to visit them in jail or at the cemetery, with us burying them instead of vice versa.

The problems we experience with guns and drugs are like any other problem, usually starting with us. While we can't move back into time, time has value. It is time to make history repeat itself. We must realize and see that before the onset of drugs the father was key in the home. Until he returns and takes the role as a teacher and monument, the family structure will disappear as well as manhood itself.

What most drug dealers don't think about when they choose to sell drugs as a way of life is that hustlers never see retirement; you hustle until you die. Uncle Sam don't pay Social Security to drug dealers and hustlers unless they pay taxes and into the Social Security Fund. Most hustlers don't pay taxes nor think about how they'll survive when they get sixty or seventy years old. The results for many are homelessness, living in shame and being a burden to others to bury us because we don't have any kind of insurance.

ANGER

With guns being the key tool in so much violence and death they become they main focus of problem, not looking at our anger for being the most volatile ingredient of our misdeeds. What we must keep in mind is that with every action there is a reaction. Almost all times a homicide or assault is committed, the assailant was angry as a reaction to something. It wasn't until taking a good look in the mirror I got the chance to see the real destructive element in my life that was leading me into obliteration. My explosive temper had almost landed me in jail a number of times from my actions while mad. Never weighing more than a hundred seventy five pounds, when becoming angry I could and would take on anyone regardless of size. For some reason I was like a Jekyl and Hyde, capable of shooting someone whose face expressed doubt. Fear wasn't in the picture. It wasn't until looking close at my prior actions, which actually made me scared of myself. Fact is many of us are the same way.

After coming close to shooting my partner and his brother I came to grips with the fact my temper was out of control. I had also shot someone who could have died from my rage. I could have spent the rest of my life in jail all because of being pissed off at someone over something material. My explosive temper was my main enemy and if something wasn't done something bad happening was inevitable. In looking at physical anger and what causes it we must ask ourselves questions as to whether anger is actually a natural instinct, more in some than others? Is it any different between men and women? Does it happen more with Black people than white? What causes it and what can we do about it? And most important, what it does to us? It is fact that almost all times a murder is committed it involves money or love; money almost all of the time in impoverished urban communities.

We must all understand that anger is an emotion, something closely related to the feminine side of our nature. One thing I find to be true in correlation to most of today's young man and myself is that there was no rational father in the household that would, by nature, teach a young man how to think instead of using emotions to settle problems. When we add emotional irrationality with use of our lower state of mind the result is a negative action instead of a positive word.

While it is impossible for one to say what exactly causes crime to be higher in one neighborhood than another, anger occurs in all neighborhoods both rich and poor and can be our own worst enemy; it will until we realize it. Whether it is over the opposite sex, money, or someone cutting in front of us on the road, the anger can easily be controlled, especially when understanding that the anger has an adverse affect on the organism creating the anger, causing other diseases in the body and a shortness of life.

We must also face the psychological effect the dollar bill has on those in poor neighborhoods as opposed to those where the bills flourish. It has been said that money is at the root of evil, and while I can't prove that, I can use myself as an example. When I came close to shooting Proctor and shot his TV it was over money. When I was set up for the rip, it was because someone wanted my money and valuables. When I shot up an innocent person's house up like a fool it was all about money they didn't even know about. When I shot Elmer J. it was because he took what was like cash and all I had. And even when I almost shot Paul and his brother, it was indirectly related to money. All times it was about money and all times anger was the fuel to set me off.

If I had been born with full pockets chances are I never would have been a dope dealer and wouldn't have sold Proc any dope in the first place. I would never have been setup for a rip because again, I wouldn't have been selling dope and my money probably would have been in a bank. And when I shot Elmer J. for taking my weed, again, I wouldn't have been selling dope in the first place.

There shouldn't be any question as to what causes so much gun violence in America today, especially in the African American neighborhoods. Drug money and anger is at the root of most crimes. If drugs had no value, there would be far fewer dead people and far fewer people making a living off those who choose the quick way and wind up in jail. While it may sound a cliché and far-fetched, if we learned to replace our anger with love and forgiveness we would heal the world within ourselves in the least.

As a mystic in many teachings I have been fortunate in making many discoveries that most don't make in a lifetime. One of these discoveries is the power of love. What we have not been taught by traditional teachings is that not only is love something that can be shared, love is esoteric, and also one of the twelve powers of man according to esoteric philosophy. Love is a power, and one of the healing elements that not only have a positive healing affect on the people it is practiced on, but more so on the person initiating the love.

Nevertheless, we believe when it comes to our money, we seem to only forgive after we get paid. Yet by holding anger and grudges, more energy is used in carrying the grudge than in forgiving the person the debt, leaving them with the guilt. We should never lose friends over money because it can be replaced, friends can't. When we can spend a few dollars to reveal one's intent it's worth it. We've learned their true nature and kept ourselves from losing a greater amount in the future.

We must understand that hate is alchemical; it can actually cause dis-ease and kill the organism through chemical imbalance. The longer hate and anger is held the more rooted it becomes, leaving the individual unable to forgive as well as love. The power of love is greater a weapon than any used with a bullet or arrow. Love is a key to start your heart; hate is the key to stop it. Love cost nothing and is the key to life. Anger takes it away. And what's most ironic, anger can be cured in most cases by simply laughing and walking away.

THE NEW DISEASE
While many may disagree who have not studied the etymology of the word, the problems of today of settling disputes with guns and anger can be classified as a disease. The term dis-ease is almost always captive in one word, disease. In prefix, dis simply means, in this case, the opposite. With our children dying in school or coming home from it, we are not at ease. When our husband or wife on a simple trip to the market or to work is shot to death for no reason at all, we are not at ease. And when someone murders our mother or father from being robbed in his or her own home, we are definitely not at ease. These types of incidents are all too

common with only a limited few not being affected directly or indirectly. Therefore, we live with a disease created by anger and guns.

As described in <u>Webster's New World Dictionary</u>, this word disease may be related to "a particular destructive process in an organ or organism, with a specific cause and characteristic of symptoms; specif., an illness; ailment." Webster goes on to describe disease as "any harmful or destructive condition, as of society." When we, as a rule, refer to this word we associate it with an illness within an individual. From a metaphysical perspective, this world is that living organism. In most cases, if uncured, dis-ease also kills the individual, us. As with most diseases, pain is also a symptom to be expected with illness. If left untreated, these symptoms may become chronic, possibly resulting in spiritual or physical fatality.

This malady has acted as a cancerous tumor attacking a global mass - slowly taking affect on the entire planet. While the warning signs are becoming more noticeable the problem has been around for quite some time. The increased drug activity and the war on drugs have contributed tremendously to this dis-ease. Though all communities are experiencing more crime and shootings than of twenty years ago, the problem of guns and anger is no longer consolidated to urban communities where there is much more dealing of drugs than in suburban areas. Now, the problem of living with and settling everything with guns is routine. With a more than average school dropout rate in poor neighborhoods comes the need to sell drugs and the inability to acquire good paying jobs, usually associated with minimum education. These individuals have found crime to be a means of survival, and it almost always involves guns.

Healing all diseases require some form of treatment. Unlike using prescription drugs to get results, the problem we have with guns and anger can be solved with education and

180 Guns, Drugs, Gangs, and Anger

the way we think. For the most part, educated people don't find themselves on the wrong side of the law. They usually know the ramifications by being cognizant of the law and the ability to maintain competitive paying jobs.

It is highly unlikely that those who have dropped out of refining themselves will pick up the habit of becoming educated. It is their descendants, our children, who can make a change. Now, the law adds to this disease even more by excluding those with minor drug convictions the gift of gaining government grants and scholarships for education that can lead them from a world of crime instead of in to one.

As it becomes obvious this carcinoma is eating the internal organs, either we make change or all die one way or another. Attacking this disease must be done by going to the root of the problem, which is the mind. If we don't change that, our attempts to cure the disease will be futile. We must truly become a kinder, gentler nation, based on a one-love ideology. No hate, no anger, with laughter being the cure. And we must look at the person in the mirror because that is where the healing process begins, but first, like any person with an illness, we must first recognize we have one.

EPILOGUE: KILLING THE ONES WE LOVE

There is usually a moral or some lesson to be taught in any story. When it comes to fighting or settling our disputes, over the last forty years things have become somewhat deadly. In the sixties we used to fight all the time, but mostly it was over girls. We'd fight about who was going to get her and after we'd beat each other's brains out the girl would wind up going with a guy that neither one of us who were fighting liked. In the end, after the bruises and black eyes healed and a few days passed, we became best of friends and sometimes where the friendship lasted for years, the two always had something to laugh about, especially when the girl wound up looking like someone we would have dread having married or something since the fight.

Seeing that I've been fortunate enough to live long enough and look back and see what some never will, in this case, the moral of this story is contrasted with the war between the Satan's Sidekicks and the Elegant Disciples. We were shooting each other over things not physically worth the value of

someone's life. Decades later we can take a look at the outcome
of things after we used brains instead of bullets.

In the agreement between the two clubs the Sidekicks
gave their word that while they could not return the colors
belonging to Elegant Disciples from allegedly being destroyed,
they gave their word they would never re-surface. In over thirty
years they never reneged on their word. And while they could
have done otherwise, they made an agreement and kept it.
That's what men are supposed to do, because their word *is*
their bond; it's the most credible thing he has.

I eventually joined the Sin City Disciples more that ten
years after the war had settled. The City was the most respected
club in the city because of its nationwide exposure as an outlaw
club. They also had a better relationship with the Kicks than the
American Motorcycle Association alliance I left. One of the few
outlaw clubs in the city, it was the only place left fit to be my
biker home. The club never had a social reputation and known
for a few problems with the law and other clubs, but when you
have hundreds of outlaws in a nationwide organization shit is
going to happen.

Once you join an outlaw club, you're usually part of that
family until you die. And they'll be the ones burying you too.
Over the years I got to know many of the Kicks who, many,
became like my own family, and Sisco had long become one
who gave me the most love whenever we saw each other. And if
I ever found myself among strangers that may have had a
vendetta with my club or just wanted to make a name the Kicks
had my back, like we had theirs. And when I needed some help
to do some construction work on my home, it was Sidekicks
that helped me do it. And with the company of a brother or two
like Chico, or Sweet Red, (*who made sure he talked enough
shit to get the job done*), how could I lose with friends like that.
And now, as our stomachs round, our heads bald and gray,
some on canes, some in wheelchairs, we now put each other to
rest as we take the final ride down heaven's highway.

It's been over thirty years since the feud between the two clubs. Good thing is the ugly part never happened because the ones who almost killed each other now save each other and know the true meaning of love. To think now that not only did we come close to killing the ones that we need in life, we came close to killing the ones we now love. But the love would have never been discovered had we not done what men are supposed to do; talk first, fight last.

EN FINALE:
AFRICAN AMERICANS AND GUN VIOLENCE

While guns, drugs, gangs, and anger exists in all communities around the globe, one fact that cannot be ignored are the statistics of gun violence among African Americans. According to statistics generated in 2005, In 2002 the gun death rate for African-American males ages 15 to 19 was 56 per 100,000, a large disparity compared to White males of the same age (14 per 100,000). For Black males ages 20-24, the gun death rate was even higher at 120 per 100,000, an even greater disparity compared to White males of the same age group (23 per 100,000).[1]

Though statistics may show that Whites, Hispanics, and others are also having a problem with the loss of their relatives and counterparts due to gun violence, we, the Black race are sacrificing more than 8 times as many than that of our cultural neighbors. When the law becomes involved, making arrests related to these homicides, the rate doubles, removing at least 240 Black folk per 100,000, leaving behind thousands of grieving friends and relatives.

Though the problem continues to grow, it's not hopeless; we can bring about a change to the ever-increasing pain of death we've learned to accept. Regardless of the many reasons for the

---

[1] ** *Numbers obtained from the CDC National Center for Health Statistics mortality report online, 2005*

cause, there are answers and ways to ease what has become routine.

As an activist in my community, I have spent many years attending and taking part in call for action groups addressing violence among young people. One common trait that repeats itself is that usually these groups are formed out of the grievance of a loved one, student, or relative. Once the tears dry, the pain eases, and the group realizes it doesn't have money or support, it slowly dissipates along with the person in memory.

What I have also found to be prevalent among these groups is that rhetoric has always replaced a realistic plan for action. For anyone to launch an attack on something there must be a course of action. It's like writing without an outline; there's no telling where you may wind up if you get anywhere and anyone else can follow it. Though there have been many ideas and non-pragmatic suggestions, none seem to be on course to driving the nails in the coffin.

I've spent many hours contemplating solutions to the growing violence. The best discovery made was that of myself. Once becoming familiar with a truer version of African history a feeling of pride became overwhelming. Whereas thinking about our history may seem irrelevant in solving the problem, it is just the opposite. I believe the loss of African pride is where our healing will begin once restored. And while slavery has been over since 1865, we still remain a displaced people speaking a foreign tongue in a non-indigenous land and without understanding. Because language advocates cultural values and religion replicates spiritual values, when someone has your language and your religion, they have you.

OUR HISTORY

I totally agree with the great elders Dr. John Henrik Clarke, and Dr. Josef Ben Jocahannan along with others who have found the history of our past being monumental in our healing. It is true that examining our past will reveal much unknown history of the Black man, which is needed for him to gain total freedom. While races other than Black are not excluded from the gun problem and share many of the same reasons, the truth is reality and the reality is our truth and can't be overlooked. The only way we can move forward is by realizing the dotted lines and connecting them.

If we paint only a scant picture depicting our African history over the last five thousand years it will give us a better perspective, which reveals how Asian/European history has left out everything dealing with Black – which was at the beginning of everything, contrary to what we have been taught about our past. In revelation of the truth not only will we find things of value that will change our position towards guns, we will discover things that will change our attitudes toward life itself – improving our prosperity as well as our achievements.

In examining our history I've used information provided by Black elders, professors and writers. I found the books *The Destruction of Black Civilization* by Chancellor Williams, ©1987, Third World Press, and *The African Origin of Civilization* by Cheikh Anta Diop, Lawrence Hill Books, ©1974 both *must reads* to trace a " more true" history of the Black race from the earliest times of recorded history. I highly recommend that anyone who considers learning about true African history read books by these authors. The references and citations of these teachers will lead to a cache of truth about Black history.

Of course modern history only teaches the "White side" of Egypt and Africa after the days the Whiteness of Asia, Arabia and Europe had infiltrated the land and stole and destroyed all history, artifacts, putting White faces on everything Black. And since many of our adversaries found it a pleasure to impregnate the women of color, a new generation of people was born. These Asians, Arabs and European mulattoes who found it a pleasure to mix with African blood still found displeasure and dislike for Black (and White), eventually creating a mindset for their offspring to discriminate against anyone of the darker people from which they came. Since that time and for different reasons, the lighter, less pigmented man has always believed he was superior over us because of his unusual color and weaponry.

Among the things still hurting the Black man is the lie he bought *suggesting* he is inferior to some other race of people on this planet. While most of us aren't as scientific as our great ancestors, it doesn't take a scientist to know that you can't get something dark from something light, but to the opposite, light is produced from darkness. There was darkness before there was light, and it took Black for White to know what *it* was. When we learn these things we will devalue all the deceit we've bought and treasured. Everything including this planet was succumb to darkness before the light, nothing excluded. It is the Anglo/European language that has associated things Black with evil and things White with good and righteous. Black became hated so much that all the Black science and Black literature was destroyed while the Black faces were turned White.

"The terms [White man] and [Black man] – which originated in England – were not introduced to classify men according to the colour of their skin, but rather to teach the populace that White is supposed to be a thing of beauty whereas Black is evil and ugly. So when they said, [Black man,] they did not just mean a man of dark skin but rather [an evil, loathsome thing,] even provoking some of their writers to literally call us demons."[2]

When we rediscover ourselves and learn about the things that make us special i.e., our knowledge, and the inherent powers everyone of all races have, we will find out the truth about Black. Until then, we will continue to buy the lie that we are less human and die believing it.

After all the discoveries, the greatest one was that of my ability and myself. Once understanding whom, what I was, and why I existed, I discovered the power and ability to do anything conceived. Understanding my Blackness became more valuable than anybody's gold. My value for life changed. There is no more racism in my world because there is none greater than me outside of my God. I don't bow down to a dollar with enslaver faces painted on them because capitalism has no consideration for the less fortunate. I am part of the world's greatest resource, Black.

The positive arrogance one inherits from higher knowledge is a fuel for acceleration. We must rediscover our past. It is there where all the secrets to life exist. When this is done our life will begin anew. The sciences we used as guides to make it through life were destroyed, hidden, or changed with their tongue to be labeled now as the "occult," because it was Black; now something everyone should stay away from, which is in part why we are lost. We must rediscover all of our sciences of life and use them. We are the original scientists and architectures of this civilization. Not only are we a great part of history, we own it. It is through reading, researching, and

---

[2] *The Destiny of the Black Race,* John Peterson

Carlisle,

gathering information that will give us the liberation to escape the reins of the things and people that still have control of our minds. It will also teach us that life wasn't meant to be based on capitalism.

In those thousands of years, through science, we set the world on the path of further scientific discovery. Religion, philosophy, chemistry, masonry and architecture, music, art, poetry, mathematics, and the list goes on including that of stellar science including that of astrology were only a few of the things we'd already mastered. By nature we've always been scientists. Our attention has been diverted and we've lost our interest along the travels. Of course it is not our fault we've had to fight so long, but now is not the time to throw in the towel. The future of Black lies in the hands of those who live today.

I know that learning the greatness of our history will also change one's value of life. Knowing I am not inferior to anyone places me in a comfortable position of not being confined with psychological constraints. We all have the choice to take the place of being whatever it is we want, not secondary to anyone because of his or her money or the color of his or her skin. We have the most valuable skin color, so what. It doesn't mean a thing if we don't have value and self-worth. Through intelligence we will discover things about ourselves the streets won't teach us. The Black man of today should be highly advanced in science instead of having problems with something insignificant as stupid guns.

In the mission to black out Black, there were insurmountable mistakes made. Continuing to live in those errors without correction perpetuates the ignorance of the guilty and places us with the knife in our own hand, cutting our own throat. Now is not time for us to give up the fight that's been ongoing for the last five thousand years. It is vital to our existence that we put our lives back together in the midst of the fight; realizing and using all the gifts and blessings that God gives us as natural ammunition.

It will be our understanding as well as an overstanding that will give us the value of who we are, which is more than guns offer or more than can be valued by a dollar or a piece of gold. As mentioned, we are the gold. It's vital for us to dig into the truth of our history and our knowledge. Of course everyone won't admire you for it because the truth hurts, but I promise you will find a new value for life. And I can't stress enough the importance of using the Black story, not his-story. If we make the common mistake and ask the person who put us in chains about our history, like the writer Chancellor Williams said, his answer is going to be, "What history? You have no history!"

The time is here for the extinction of many people on this planet. We must not welcome it. There are many methods of extermination being used to Whiteout Black, as it has been for the last five thousand years i.e., AIDS, drugs, and guns. And while those of us living probably won't see our end, if we don't do something to change our course from destruction, our great grandchildren could be the ones to write the last history books of this civilization.

Hotep, ˜ Peace Be With You ˜

During the last days of finishing this book Maurice O'Sheen
Sisco, a.k.a. "Sisco Kidd" took his final ride.

You are forever in all our memories.

S.F.F.S.

5/8/1950 – 9/9/2012

"Thanks for the love and dedication of inspiring our young
people to higher education no matter the walk of life."

20198975R00110

Made in the USA
Lexington, KY
24 January 2013